A. PHILIP RANDOLPH

The **African-American Biographies** Series

—African-American Biographies—

A. PHILIP RANDOLPH

Union Leader and Civil Rights Crusader

Series Consultant:
Dr. Russell L. Adams, Chairman
Department of Afro-American Studies, Howard University

Catherine Reef

Enslow Publishers, Inc.

40 Industrial Road   PO Box 38
Box 398   Aldershot
Berkeley Heights, NJ 07922   Hants GU12 6BP
USA   UK

http://www.enslow.com

Library of Congress Cataloging-in-Publication Data

Reef, Catherine.
    A. Philip Randolph : union leader and civil rights crusader / Catherine
Reef.
        p. cm. — (African-American biographies)
    Includes bibliographical references and index.
    ISBN 0-7660-1544-0
    1. Randolph, A. Philip (Asa Philip), 1889–1979—Juvenile literature.
2. Afro-Americans—Biography—Juvenile literature. 3. Civil rights
workers—United States—Biography—Juvenile literature. 4. Labor
unions—United States—Officials and employees—Biography—Juvenile
literature. 5. Brotherhood of Sleeping Car Porters—History—Juvenile
literature. 6. Afro-Americans—Civil rights—History—Juvenile literature.
7. Civil rights movements—United States—History—20th century—
Juvenile literature. [1. Randolph, A. Philip (Asa Philip), 1889–1979.
2. Civil rights workers. 3. Afro-Americans—Biography. 4. Brotherhood of
Sleeping Car Porters—History.] I. Title. II. Series.
E185.97.R27 R44   2001
323'.092—dc21
                                    00-009784

To Our Readers: All Internet Addresses in this book were active and appropriate
when we went to press. Any comments or suggestions can be sent by e-mail to
Comments@enslow.com or to the address on the back cover.

Photo Credits: A. Philip Randolph Institute, 40; Betsy Graves Reyneau
(1888–1964), oil on canvas, National Portrait Gallery, Smithsonian
Institution, p. 6; Chicago Historical Society, DN-71301, Chicago Daily
News, p. 52; General Commission on Archives and History, the United
Methodist Church, p. 28; Library of Congress, pp. 10, 17, 35, 38, 59, 64,
74, 82, 87, 91, 95, 99, 112; National Archives, p. 50; Tebeau-Field
Library of Florida History, Cocoa, Florida, p. 22; Walter P. Reuther
Library, Wayne State University, pp., 8, 107; Walter P. Reuther Library,
Wayne State University, © Wide World Photos, p. 110.

Cover Photo: Betsy Graves Reyneau (1888–1964), oil on canvas,
National Portrait Gallery, Smithsonian Institution

Contents

A. Philip Randolph

1

ONE MAN'S DREAM

The temperature reached into the eighties on August 28, 1963. In a city where summer highs of ninety degrees or more were common, it was a pleasant day—a fine day for marching.

More than two hundred thousand people had assembled in the nation's capital to demonstrate for equal rights for African Americans. They were black and white, old and young. Many had traveled long distances, from Alabama, Florida, New York, Michigan, and other states. They had journeyed by bus, car, train, and plane to be part of history, part of the March on Washington for Jobs and Freedom.

Leaders of the 1963 March on Washington lock hands as they demonstrate for jobs and freedom for African Americans. A. Philip Randolph stands second from right. Next to him, from right to left, are Walter Reuther of the United Auto Workers, then Roy Wilkins of the NAACP and Whitney M. Young, Jr., of the National Urban League.

A. Philip Randolph stood atop the high marble steps of the Lincoln Memorial and surveyed the mass of people. He was a lean, tall man. Age had whitened his hair, but he stood straight and proud. This great march had long been his dream. He had helped to make it happen.

The New York Times reported that the March on

Washington capped a civil rights movement that was three and a half years old. The newspaper measured the civil rights years from February 1960. That was when students from the Negro Agricultural and Technical College in Greensboro, North Carolina, ordered food at a whites-only lunch counter and sat all day without being served.

The period known as the civil rights era actually began in the 1950s, though. In 1954, the Supreme Court outlawed segregation in public schools. In 1955 and 1956, residents of Montgomery, Alabama, staged a boycott to end seating according to race on the city's buses.

African Americans were challenging segregation wherever it was practiced. In 1962, for example, James Meredith became the first African American to enroll in the University of Mississippi. Meredith defied a tradition of racial separation so strong that he needed the protection of federal forces to enter the school. In the spring of 1963, the men, women, and children of Birmingham, Alabama, endured police-dog attacks and blasts from fire hoses as they demonstrated for jobs and fair treatment in the city where they lived.

But A. Philip Randolph had been working to create opportunities for African Americans for nearly forty years. In 1925—before Martin Luther King, Jr., was even born—Randolph organized the Brotherhood of Sleeping Car Porters. The Brotherhood was a labor union for the African Americans who served passengers on railway sleeping cars. He took on this task at a time when most labor unions restricted their membership to whites. It was a time when the porters worked longer hours and earned less money than whites employed in train travel.

During World War II, Randolph worked to create opportunities for African Americans in defense plants. In 1947 and 1948, he led protests against segregation in the armed forces. Until Randolph took action,

Randolph traveled to many other nations in the years following World War II. Here he meets with officers of a railway workers' union in Rangoon, Burma. Randolph is seated at right, facing left.

blacks could not serve their country as the equals of whites.

Bayard Rustin, Randolph's longtime assistant, observed in 1979 that Randolph's "leadership flowed from the depth of his humanity. It flowed from his understanding of the human condition."[1] Rustin called Randolph "the most effective and most gentle man I shall ever know. Mr. Randolph was a man I never heard, in 40 years of working with him, say an unkind word about any individual—foe or friend."[2]

Speaking from the Lincoln Memorial on August 28, 1963, Randolph welcomed the people attending the march. "We are gathered here in the largest demonstration in the history of the nation," he said.[3] He let it be known that this march was a fresh start for the African-American people, saying, "We are the advanced guard of a massive moral revolution for jobs and freedom." He pictured this revolution rolling across the land, "touching every city, every town, every village where black men are segregated, oppressed and exploited."[4] A reporter who was present compared Randolph's voice to the soft, deep tones played on an organ.

In his speech, Randolph called for a national commitment to making good jobs available to all Americans who were willing to work hard. He mentioned the other goals of the march: passage of a civil rights law and integrated public schools. Too many

African-American children still attended inferior, segregated schools in 1963.

Randolph continued, "The march on Washington is not the climax to our struggle but a new beginning, not only for the Negro but for all Americans, for personal freedoms and a better life."[5]

The crowd listened that afternoon to speeches by

President Lyndon B. Johnson presents the Medal of Freedom—the nation's highest civilian honor—to A. Philip Randolph on September 14, 1964.

younger leaders as well. John Lewis of the Student Nonviolent Coordinating Committee (SNCC) called on politicians to take a stand on matters of principle. He asked African Americans to continue their protests in a spirit of dignity. Roy Wilkins of the National Association for the Advancement of Colored People (NAACP) deplored the violent treatment of civil rights workers in the South and the government's failure to protect them. Whitney M. Young, Jr., of the National Urban League urged the nation to create a future free of discrimination, dedicated to justice and brotherhood. The final speaker of the day was the Reverend Martin Luther King, Jr. For the first time, the world heard his most famous words: "I have a dream . . ."[6]

Later in the day, when the speeches were over and the crowd was breaking up, Randolph stood again at the Lincoln Memorial, looking out. Bayard Rustin put an arm around the older man's shoulder and said, "Mr. Randolph, it looks like your dream has come true."[7]

"And when I looked into his eyes," Rustin said, "I could see that tears were streaming down his cheeks."[8] It was the only time Rustin saw Randolph unable to hold back his feelings.

2

PREACHER'S SON

When James and Elizabeth Randolph's second son was born, on April 15, 1889, they named him Asa, after a ruler of the ancient kingdom of Judah in the Holy Land. According to the Old Testament, King Asa rid his land of idol worship. He was faithful to the Hebrew god, Yahweh, all his life.

The Randolphs knew the Bible well. James Randolph was a poor minister in the African Methodist Episcopal Church who preached in Crescent City, Florida. Born in 1864, he was descended from slaves owned by the wealthy Randolphs of Virginia, who were related to Thomas Jefferson. Asa's father had grown up in Monticello, Florida, where he attended a school for African Americans run by northern missionaries. He was trained to be a tailor, but his interest lay in Bible study. By age twenty, he was an ordained minister preaching in the small town of Baldwin, Florida.

In Baldwin he met tall, beautiful Elizabeth Robinson. The two were married in 1885, and their first son, James Randolph, Jr., was born in 1887.

When James was four and Asa Philip was two, the family moved to Jacksonville, Florida. There, the Reverend Randolph became minister of a small congregation.

The thriving port of Jacksonville is on the Atlantic Coast at the mouth of the St. Johns River. Ships departing from Jacksonville in the 1890s carried cotton and lumber. The cotton was raised on farms throughout the South; the lumber came from the pine and oak forests that grew outside the city. Tourism was big business in Jacksonville as well. White northerners who liked the warm Florida climate filled Jacksonville's hotels from January through April. They went sailing and horseback riding. In the souvenir shops on Bay Street, they bought heron feathers, whistles carved from alligator teeth, and hats fashioned from palmetto leaves.

Asa Randolph grew up in an unusual southern city, one where African Americans held positions of responsibility. There were African-American police officers and city council members, as well as an African-American fire company. There was even an African-American judge on the municipal court.

Long gray strands of Spanish moss hung from the live oaks that shaded downtown Jacksonville and the wealthy suburbs. Housing in Jacksonville was largely segregated in 1891, although some blacks and whites lived in mixed neighborhoods. Most African Americans lived in communities such as Oakland, the tough part of town where the Randolphs settled.

The family grew fruits and vegetables in their yard, and they raised hogs and chickens. Their home was small and simply furnished, and Elizabeth Randolph kept it spotless. She was a serious, hardworking woman who rarely took time to visit friends. Like her husband, she was deeply religious.

Asa's parents did tailoring and cleaned clothes to earn a few extra dollars each week. For a while, the Reverend Randolph ran a meat market. Later on, he tried selling firewood. (Most of Jacksonville's African Americans burned wood to heat their homes and cook their food.) But Asa's father had little talent for business, and both ventures failed. He even wound up owing money to the wholesaler who had supplied him with wood. As an adult, A. Philip Randolph recalled that his father "had to scuffle for a long time to pay off the debt."[1]

Like most rural African-American ministers, the

Here in Jacksonville, Florida, in the early twentieth century, many residents depended on streetcars for transportation.

Reverend Randolph preached to several congregations. Once a month, he delivered a sermon in Baldwin. He also made monthly trips to the villages of Palatka and Green Cove Springs to conduct church services there. When Asa grew old enough, his father took him along. Father and son traveled up the St. Johns River on a steamboat and spent the night with church members. "I liked these trips because I had the run of the houses where we visited," A. Philip Randolph remembered.[2] "My mother would have scolded me for some of the things I did on these visits," Randolph added, "but my father was very indulgent."[3]

The Reverend Randolph was a gentle father but a demanding teacher. He taught his sons about African-American heroes such as Crispus Attucks (c. 1723–1770), the first person to die in the Boston Massacre, which was one of the conflicts that led to American Revolution; François Dominique Toussaint L'Ouverture (1743–1803), who led the struggle for independence in Haiti; and Frederick Douglass (1817–1895), the escaped slave who spoke and wrote against slavery.

He also taught them about Bishop Henry McNeal Turner (1834–1915) of the African Methodist Episcopal Church. In earlier years, Turner had been a lion of the church, Randolph said. He was a forceful man "who shook his mane and roared and thundered against slavery."[4] Turner was the first African-American army chaplain during the Civil War. After the war, he founded African Methodist Episcopal churches in Georgia and other states and brought thousands of people into the faith. Turner was an out-spoken critic of racism who shocked white America when he proclaimed, "God is a Negro."[5] Convinced that his people could never achieve equality in the United States, Turner urged American blacks to move to Africa. He made four trips to Africa himself between 1891 and 1898, but he never settled there.

The Randolph brothers met Henry McNeal Turner at an African Methodist Episcopal convention that was held in Jacksonville. The fiery bishop embraced Asa and James and told them that they were fine boys.

Still, there was more to Asa's childhood than learning and religion. "Though far from a gay, happy-go-lucky, little fellow, I enjoyed certain forms of play . . . ," he later wrote.[6] Asa played baseball and ran races. He enjoyed games of marbles and hide-and-seek with Beaman Hearn, a boy who lived across the street. Hearn remembered that Asa often had his nose in a book, because the Reverend Randolph insisted that his sons read every day. They were free to choose from the family's small collection of books, which included works by the great English writers William Shakespeare, Jane Austen, and Charles Dickens. Asa sometimes read sermons aloud, mimicking his father's rich speaking voice.

Asa's best friend was his brother. "We were always together as boys," A. Philip Randolph said. "I loved my brother very much."[7] Although Asa was two years younger than James, they started school together and were in the same grade. Both boys earned good marks, but James was the star pupil. James also had a hot temper and was quick to pick fights with boys much larger than himself. Asa, who hated to fight, could not stand by and let James take a beating alone. Both boys suffered many bruises and cut lips, but they won Elizabeth Randolph's approval. "If we went home with blackened eyes and reported that we were in a fight, we would be whipped again by our mother unless we convinced her that we fought back," A. Philip Randolph said. "She made it unmistakably clear that she hated a coward."[8]

The lynching of an African American was a far more serious event than a schoolyard brawl. Lynching is a form of murder. The victim is executed by his or her fellow citizens without standing trial. In the United States, most lynchings have been rooted in racism. More than thirty-three hundred African-American men were reported lynched between 1882 and 1930. Historians suspect that the actual total is higher.

A. Philip Randolph recalled that a lynching nearly occurred in Jacksonville when he was growing up. Randolph never said exactly when this happened, but the events he described match those that took place on July 4, 1892. On that date, a black man named Ben Reed was arrested for killing a white man in a fight.

Randolph remembered that some local whites were planning to take the black prisoner from the county jail and lynch him. The Reverend Randolph joined a crowd of armed black men who spent the night guarding the jail to chase would-be lynchers away. Elizabeth Randolph, who was an expert shot, sat on the front porch at home with a loaded shotgun in her lap in case there was trouble. "It gave us a wonderful feeling to know that Mother could protect the home when Father was away," Randolph said.[9]

Fearing racial violence in the case of Ben Reed,

the governor of Florida ordered militia forces to Jacksonville to keep the peace. Because the soldiers avoided using force and community leaders of both races kept the people calm, there was no real trouble. Ben Reed was tried for his crime and sentenced to four years in prison.

For Asa Randolph and all the citizens of Jacksonville, May 3, 1901, was another unforgettable day. At 12:30 P.M. on that day, a spark from a cooking fire landed on a pile of Spanish moss that had been left to dry outside the Cleaveland Fibre Factory. (In the nineteenth century, people used Spanish moss to cushion breakable items in packages and to stuff upholstered furniture.) Bits of burning moss ignited the factory building, and then wind carried the fire to nearby structures.

The *Florida Times-Union and Citizen* reported that houses "burned like cigar boxes, like chaff, as the thundering, mighty, lurid storm-wave of fire rolled to the east, ever to the east, and swept the area bare."[10] The fire destroyed churches, stores, and an orphanage. "Beautiful home after home became a torch, its light lost in the monstrous mass of red illumination."[11] People as far away as Savannah, Georgia, saw the flames, and residents of Raleigh, North Carolina, reported seeing the smoke.

Some of Jacksonville's citizens crowded into the Western Union office to send telegrams to loved ones as buildings across the street burned to the ground. Others packed their belongings into wagons and hurried to safety. The fire spread so fast that firefighters could do little to stop it. It was only after the wind died down, at 7:30 that evening, that the fire was contained. The death toll was low—seven people. But 2,368 buildings, including 1,700 homes, were destroyed.

The Randolphs's Oakland neighborhood was spared, and its residents pitched in to help shelter the homeless. Donations of food, clothing, bedding, tools, and money arrived from communities all over the

The fire of 1901 spread to the Jacksonville waterfront, where it destroyed piers and vessels.

country. By May 6, three days after the fire, the people of Jacksonville were already rebuilding their city.

It seemed to many African Americans that the fire-fighters had tried harder to save the houses of whites than the homes of black families. Racial tension resulted, and it grew even worse after November 6, 1901. That was when the city council passed an ordinance requiring blacks and whites to sit in separate sections on streetcars.

Since the 1880s, southern states and cities had been enacting laws designed to keep the races apart. These laws, known as "Jim Crow" laws, prevented blacks from mingling with whites in hotels and on trains, in schools and in theaters. In 1896, the U.S. Supreme Court upheld this kind of segregation in deciding the case known as *Plessy* v. *Ferguson*. The Court permitted segregation as long as the facilities provided for blacks and whites were "separate but equal." Few facilities for blacks equaled those available to whites, though. Even Duval County, Florida, where Jacksonville was located, spent $12.08 to educate each white child in 1900 and only $5.47 to educate each black child.

As Jim Crow laws took effect in Jacksonville, African Americans lost their high-level positions and much of the freedom they had enjoyed. The Reverend Randolph refused to obey these demeaning laws. He stopped riding in streetcars. After the public library set aside a separate reading room for African Americans, he no longer visited the library. Despite the fact that he wanted his sons to read, he insisted that they follow his example. The library was now off-limits for Asa and James. And every morning and afternoon, instead of riding the streetcar, they walked the long distance between home and school.

3

COMING INTO
HIS OWN

In 1903, when Asa was fourteen, he and James enrolled in the Cookman Institute, a high school founded by Methodist missionaries after the Civil War. Cookman was the first high school for African Americans in Florida, and for years it was the only one. Its first students included many former slaves. In those days, old men and women learned alongside young people in day and evening classes.

Some of the boys and girls attending the Cookman Institute with Asa and James Randolph trained to be teachers. Others took courses that prepared them for college. The school offered classes in biology and chemistry, music and drama, literature, mathematics, foreign languages, and public speaking. There were also classes in sewing and domestic science, which is the study of household management. Because Cookman was a church-run school, the students received instruction in religion and morals as well.

Education was a topic of lively debate in the African-American community when Asa Randolph was growing up. Booker T. Washington, a leading spokesperson for African Americans, thought that the young people of his race should learn a trade. He said that blacks could best gain acceptance in white society by performing useful, if lowly, tasks. In 1881, Washington had founded the Tuskegee Institute, a school that taught African Americans such skills as farming, repairing machinery, and making cheese and butter. The school also taught students how to be household servants, carpenters, and dressmakers. Washington advised black Americans to "cast down your bucket where you are," to do work that met with whites' approval, and to avoid trying to move up in society too quickly.[1]

Most African Americans in the South earned a meager living as sharecroppers and had little chance for education. Although a school like the Tuskegee Institute allowed them to improve their prospects, some other African-American leaders criticized Washington for trying to please whites.

W. E. B. Du Bois, the brilliant professor of history and economics at Atlanta University, urged African Americans to assert their rights and achieve full equality. He pointed out that some blacks, just like some whites, had the potential to be scientists, writers, and scholars. Teaching them to labor with their hands would waste their talents. He called for "the education of youth according to ability."[2] A well-rounded education was most important, he said, for the "Talented Tenth," the brightest young people who were the future leaders of the African-American community.[3]

By entering the Cookman Institute, Asa Randolph "came into my own," he said.[4] Two of his teachers, Lillie M. Whitney and Mary Neff, noticed that he had plenty of ability. With their encouragement, he stepped out of James's shadow and excelled in his courses. He was one of the best singers in the school choir and a key player on the Cookman baseball team. Asa was popular with both the teachers and the students. He was a polite, quiet boy who dressed neatly and was considerate of others. When he shot up to be six feet tall, he acquired the nickname "String Bean."

At home, Asa talked over the issues of the day with his father and brother. "Ours was a home of ideas," Randolph explained. "While the home was not full of

Asa Randolph attended high school here at the Cookman Institute.

fabulous furniture, it was full of conversation."[5] The three had many discussions about the role of African Americans in society—discussions that made the boys think about what their own future roles would be. A. Philip Randolph said, "My brother and I dreamed of doing many things, of leading the fight for human rights as congressmen, or working as educators, scientists, doctors and writers. . . ."[6]

The Randolphs talked, too, about the fact that throughout the South, African Americans were denied the right to vote. They talked about the migration of

African Americans to the West and North that had begun to occur. The desire to exercise their rights as citizens and the danger of racial violence had prompted many people to leave the South. The exodus included community leaders—businesspeople, doctors, lawyers, and teachers—as well as ordinary working men and women.

Thousands of African Americans from the Southeast had moved to Kansas and other midwestern states in the hope of creating a better life. Nearly fifteen thousand African Americans went to Kansas in 1879 and 1880. The promise of opportunity drew thousands of others to the Northeast, especially to New York. More than forty-three thousand African Americans from the South Atlantic states settled in New York State between 1880 and 1910. Most of them made their home in New York City. They were joined by a large number of West Indian immigrants seeking jobs and education.

Asa's cousin William had left Florida to settle in New York City. Asa spent one summer vacation in New York and worked alongside William, who was a janitor, to earn some spending money. The big city was noisy and exciting, and it promised greater freedom than was to be found in the South. Asa bought stylish clothes and tickets to the theater. Some of the hit shows in New York at that time contained tunes by Cole and Johnson Brothers, an African-American songwriting team. Composer Bob Cole was a native of Georgia. The Johnson brothers, James Weldon Johnson and J. Rosamond Johnson, were from Jacksonville.

Asa returned to Florida and his studies at summer's end. In the spring of 1907, he and James graduated from the Cookman Institute. As class valedictorian— the student with the highest grades—Asa addressed the other new graduates and their families. He gave a speech titled "The Man of the Hour," about the future he envisioned for African Americans.

Some members of the class went on to college, but the Randolphs had no money to pay for further education. Despite their dreams of future achievement, Asa and James had to earn a paycheck. James worked at the post office, while Asa moved from one job to another over the next four years. He worked in a grocery store, and he knocked on people's doors to collect payments due on their insurance policies. For a time, he was a railroad section hand. This exhausting job required him to lay wooden ties and iron rails for train tracks and to shovel dirt and load railroad cars with sand.

A smart young man who wanted to use his mind gained no satisfaction from jobs such as these. Asa still read often, and he joined a theater group that performed plays for local audiences. His deep voice served him so well as an actor that people in the last rows of the theater could easily hear his lines. The

Reverend Randolph knew of another way for Asa to use that stirring voice. "In my youth my father and bishops of his church brought great pressure to bear on me to become a preacher," Randolph stated, "but I was not greatly impressed."[7] Asa lacked the strong religious beliefs that his parents held.

Around 1910, Asa Randolph read a book that altered the course of his life. It was *The Souls of Black Folk*, by W. E. B. Du Bois, which was first published in 1903. This important collection of essays contained Du Bois's criticism of Booker T. Washington. But Du Bois also wrote about other subjects, including spirituals and the African-American church, poverty and the history of his people since slavery. Du Bois put into words how it felt to be black in the United States and never fully accepted by the white majority. He wrote, "One ever feels his two-ness—an American, a Negro; two souls, two thoughts, two unreconciled strivings. . . ."[8] He predicted that in the century just beginning, African Americans would need to break down the barriers that kept them from achieving equality. "The problem of the twentieth century," he stated, "is the problem of the color line."[9]

Asa Randolph finished Du Bois's book convinced that it was "absolutely necessary to fight for social equality."[10] He began to think that he would conduct this noble battle on the national front, far from the shaded, segregated streets of Jacksonville.

In 1911, when he was twenty-two years old, Asa Randolph boarded a steamboat with his childhood friend Beaman Hearn to spend the summer in New York City. The two young men worked in the ship's galley to help pay their way. The cramped, dirty conditions in which the kitchen help lived shocked Randolph. "It was like Hades to me," he admitted, and he vowed never to work in such surroundings again.[11]

Hearn went back to Florida at summer's end to take a job selling fruits and vegetables, but Randolph remained in New York. He would never return to Jacksonville to live.

4

SOCIALIST

sa Randolph settled in Harlem, a neighborhood in the northern part of Manhattan. A few years earlier, most of Harlem's residents had been white. Now, blacks were moving there in growing numbers. People arrived filled with hope, dreams, and ideas, eager to build a community. The African Americans of Harlem founded churches, businesses, and civic organizations.

Randolph tasted the excitement of life in Harlem as he walked along Lenox Avenue and Seventh Avenue, two busy thoroughfares. At street corners, he listened to fervent speeches about politics and racial equality.

Eager to enter the debate, Randolph joined the Epworth League, a Bible group for young adults that met in a Harlem church. He sat quietly at the meetings until there was a lull in the conversation; then he steered the discussion to politics. The talks were lively, but Randolph grew impatient with the other group members and their old-fashioned notions. Like Booker T. Washington, they favored gradual progress toward racial equality. They called Randolph a troublemaker because he heeded W. E. B. Du Bois's call for action.

Randolph also joined the church drama club and performed in scenes from Shakespeare's plays. He learned to say his lines with a cultured accent, and he liked that way of speaking so much that he began to use it all the time. He wrote to his parents that he was thinking of a career as an actor, but he gave up the stage when they disapproved of that plan. The Reverend and Mrs. Randolph declared that the son of a clergyman ought to choose a more dignified profession.

To buy food and pay his rent, Randolph worked at a string of low-paying jobs, as he had done in Jacksonville. He was an elevator operator, a dishwasher, and a floor cleaner. For a time, he was a porter for the Consolidated Edison Company, the firm that supplied New York City with electricity.

Randolph also went back to school. A friend from

A stylishly dressed A. Philip Randolph, circa 1911, soon after he arrived in New York City.

the Epworth League told him that the City College of New York was free to students who met the entrance requirements. Because he had a high school diploma and had earned good grades, Randolph was sure to get in. He enrolled in the college and took classes in public speaking, history, economics, and political science. At City College, he met men and women his own age who explored new ways of thinking. He withdrew from the Epworth League and helped to found a student discussion group called the Independent Political Council.

Many of Randolph's new friends rejected capitalism, which is the economic system that operates in the United States. They thought that as long as the means of production and distribution—things like factories, mines, and railroads—belonged to private citizens, there would be inequality. They claimed that capitalists profited at the expense of workers, who endured poverty and suffering. These students embraced another economic system, socialism, which calls for industries and public services to be owned cooperatively by all citizens.

Some Socialists preached that abolishing capitalism would put black workers on an equal footing with whites. "The Negro, given economic freedom, will not ask the white man any social favors; and the burning question of 'social equality' will disappear like mist before the sunrise," said Eugene Debs, who ran for president five times as the Socialist Party candidate between 1900 and 1920.[1] Debs also said, "The Socialist Party is the party of the working class, regardless of color. . . ."[2] Statements such as these convinced Randolph that socialism could benefit African Americans. He committed himself to the Socialist cause.

Socialists viewed labor unions as a weapon against capitalism. Workers who banded together in unions gained bargaining power. Acting as a group, they could approach their employers to demand better working conditions and more money. By forcing employers to meet those demands, the Socialists thought, workers robbed the capitalists of strength.

In January 1912, the students at City College followed the news from Lawrence, Massachusetts, where three thousand textile-mill workers had walked off the job to protest a cut in wages. The strikers demanded not only a return to their old pay rate, which was already low, but a raise as well. The Industrial Workers of the World (IWW), a radical labor organization that was bent on destroying the capitalist system, was directing the strike. Soon, twenty thousand mill workers in other Massachusetts towns joined the walkout. The strike turned violent when police, acting on behalf of the wealthy mill owners, attacked innocent people. One woman died in the rioting that occurred. Some mill owners planted dynamite in local businesses and

Children of Lawrence, Massachusetts, march in New York City to aid the striking textile workers. Many parents sent their children away from Lawrence during the strike to protect them from possible violence.

planned to blame any explosions on the IWW, but their plot was exposed. The strike was a test of wills. The public waited to see who would hold out longer, management or the workers.

The strike ended in a victory for the workers. On March 12, the American Woolen Company, the largest employer in Lawrence, agreed to increase wages and to pay an extra 25 percent ("time-and-a-quarter") for overtime work.

Randolph was inspired to organize his own labor protest when he took a job as a waiter aboard the *Paul Revere*, a steamboat that traveled between New York and Boston. Once again, he encountered hellish working conditions—a dank, stinking galley and cramped, dirty living quarters. The bosses caught Randolph persuading coworkers to stand up to management, and they fired him before he had completed his first round-trip.

In New York, Randolph wrote pamphlets for the Brotherhood of Labor, an agency that found jobs for African Americans. The building that housed the Brotherhood of Labor also contained a beauty salon. Randolph soon got to know the owner of the beauty shop, a young widow named Lucille Campbell Green.

At first it seemed as though the two had nothing in common. Green was financially well off and went to parties hosted by rich friends, including Madam C. J. Walker. Walker had earned a fortune developing and selling hair-care products for African-American women. She owned a chain of beauty salons, and she had founded a school for beauticians. Lucille Green was one of the school's first graduates.

Randolph shunned high society and allied himself with the working masses. But he found Lucille Green to be generous and caring. She shared his love of Shakespeare, his commitment to helping others, and

Lucille Green, Randolph's future wife.

even his birthday. Asa Randolph, who had never had a girlfriend before, took Lucille Green to movies and political lectures. He and Lucille called each other "Buddy," and in November 1914, they were married.

Lucille Randolph earned enough money from her business to support the couple, which meant that Asa could stop working at menial jobs and devote himself to his studies. Lucille introduced her husband to Chandler Owen, a Columbia University student with a passion for politics, and the two men forged a close friendship. They made an odd pair. Owen was cynical while Randolph was formal and polite, and Owen had fantasies about being rich that Randolph would never share. But throughout his life, Randolph looked beneath the surface to form his opinions of people. In Chandler Owen he found someone dedicated to socialism and to helping his race.

Randolph and Owen spent hours reading political tracts and discussing the authors' ideas. By late 1916, they had done enough reading and were ready for action. They dropped out of college and joined the Socialist Party. They also became two of Harlem's noisy sidewalk orators. Randolph always drew a crowd when he stood at the corner of Lenox Avenue and 135th Street making speeches. Listeners—especially young people—could not wait to hear what he would say next. He and Owen were "on an uncharted sea," Randolph said. "Chandler and I had no job and no plan for the next meal."[3] Of course, they had Lucille Randolph's financial support.

One of the people who listened to Randolph and Owen speak was William White, president of a union of African-American hotel waiters. In January 1917, White hired the pair to produce a new magazine for the union members. He gave them the freedom to write and print whatever they chose. Asa Randolph began to use the professional-sounding name A. Philip Randolph on the articles that he wrote.

Randolph and Owen produced eight issues of the magazine, which was called the *Hotel Messenger*. In August 1917, they learned that freedom of the press, as William White defined it, had limits. That month, they published an article exposing the fact that some headwaiters were pocketing illegal profits from the sale of uniforms to their staffs. The article enraged William White. The headwaiters were among the most important members of his union, and he had no intention of angering them. He immediately fired his writers.

Eager to start a new project, Randolph and Owen decided to publish a magazine of their own. It was called the *Messenger*, and it was produced with Lucille Randolph's financial backing. The first issue appeared in November 1917. It proclaimed itself to be the "only magazine of scientific radicalism in the world published by Negroes."[4] By "scientific radicalism" the editors meant radical politics, especially socialism.

In the first issue of the *Messenger*, the editors stated that the magazine "is written in a fine style; its matter is logically presented . . . without prejudice in favor of the Negro or against the White Man."[5] In that issue and the ones that followed, they called on African Americans to play an active role in the political and social life of the nation.

The *Messenger* urged African-American workers to form labor unions. Randolph and Owen wrote, "Negro workers especially suffer from low wages, long hours and bad conditions under which to work. . . . Having thoroughly organized, they should make a united demand for more wages, shorter hours and better conditions."[6] African-American farmers would do well to organize, too, Randolph and Owen said, in order to command higher prices for their produce.

The two editors also told their readers that "Negroes must get into the Socialist Party."[7] They explained their reasoning: "Socialism is the political party of the working people. Now 99 per cent. of the Negroes are working people, so they should join the working people's party."[8] The Socialist Party, they said, "draws no race, creed, color or nationality lines. All are freely welcome into its ranks."[9]

Articles in the *Messenger* described how socialism would benefit the United States. One article claimed that government ownership of the railroads would ensure that food and manufactured goods reached the poor and hungry. In another piece, Randolph wrote that southern capitalists encouraged poor whites to be prejudiced against blacks. By keeping the workers divided, employers prevented them from joining together to demand better working conditions. Racial discord protected industry's profits.

The only way to rid the nation of lynching, poverty, and other problems, said Randolph, was to learn why they existed. "Because in order to remove the effects of a disease, physical or social, you must first remove the cause," he wrote.[10] To the editors of the *Messenger*, the cause of America's ills was capitalism.

5

Dangerous!

In 1917 and 1918, the *Messenger* talked about patriotism. It was a new kind of patriotism that "sees the Negro at the front bearing the brunt of almost every war in the country's history."[1] War and patriotism were on many people's minds because in April 1917, the United States had entered World War I.

Since the start of the twentieth century, the countries of Europe had been forming alliances and threatening one another with attack. One cause of dispute was the fate of Bosnia, part of Serbia. The people there wanted to be free from Austro-Hungarian rule. On June 28, 1914, a Serbian assassin shot and killed Archduke Franz Ferdinand of Austria and touched off a war. The dispute quickly grew into the global conflict now known as World War I. Austria-Hungary, Germany, and Turkey banded together as the Central Powers. Together they fought against the Allies: France, Great Britain, Russia, Serbia, and Belgium.

As a neutral nation, the United States worked to find a peaceful solution to the crisis. But the American efforts failed. In January 1917, Germany announced its intent to wage submarine warfare against any ships traveling to and from Great Britain. To President Woodrow Wilson, Germany's threat violated the right of U.S. shipping firms to do business freely. Within months, Wilson went before Congress to request a declaration of war.

Most Americans—and, indeed, most African Americans—supported the war effort. The world situation appeared so ominous that W. E. B. Du Bois encouraged African Americans to postpone their struggle for equality until after victory was achieved. He wrote, "Let us, while this war lasts, forget our special grievances and close our ranks shoulder to shoulder with our own white fellow citizens and the allied nations that are fighting for democracy."[2]

Approximately 367,000 African Americans served overseas in the armed forces, and many showed great bravery. Privates Henry Johnson and Needham

Roberts of the 369th Infantry, an African-American unit, were the first U.S. soldiers to receive the Croix de Guerre (the "war cross"), a French military medal. (Blacks and whites had served in separate units in the U.S. military for most of the nation's history.)

Like many Socialists, A. Philip Randolph opposed U.S. entry into the war. The Socialist Party took the position that the war benefited manufacturers, who profited from the sale of weapons, airplanes, and military tanks. The Socialists also objected to fighting a war to protect the interests of the shipping industry. Randolph and Owen stated in the *Messenger* that "those who profit from the war ought to pay for it."[3]

Randolph also insisted that African-American soldiers should not risk their lives to bring democracy to Europe when they were denied freedom at home. He and Owen wrote, "It should be explained to [the African-American soldier] how his economic, political and social condition will be improved by the sacrifice which he is making in the world blood-bath."[4] The *Messenger* objected as well to W. E. B. Du Bois's call for unity with whites. Du Bois's statement "will rank in shame and reeking disgrace," the editors predicted.[5]

It was a risky time to print words of protest. The government, worried about spying and dissent, had enacted laws restricting Americans' freedom of speech and expression. The Espionage Act of 1917 gave the postmaster power to halt the mailing of any publication deemed objectionable. The Sedition Act of 1918 made it a crime to say, write, or print anything critical of the government or the armed forces.

Because Randolph and Owen went ahead and published antiwar literature, government agents watched them constantly. Randolph and Owen were convinced that the Justice Department had ordered searches of their office. More than once they opened their door in the morning to find furniture smashed, papers strewn across the floor, and copies of their magazine gone. The post office revoked their second-class mailing privileges, requiring them to mail the *Messenger* at the costlier first-class rate.

In August 1918, Randolph and Owen traveled to Cleveland, Ohio, to speak to an African-American audience about socialism and to sell copies of the *Messenger*. While Randolph was making his speech, an agent of the Justice Department barged into the hall and arrested the two men.

The editors of the *Messenger* could have received sentences of twenty years in prison for their antiwar activities, or they could have been fined $10,000. But when they went to trial, the judge's racism worked in their favor. The judge found it hard to believe that African Americans could understand socialism well enough to write the articles in the *Messenger*. He suspected that white Socialists had really published the magazine and enlisted Randolph and Owen to distribute it. The judge dismissed the charges against the two men and told them to get out of town.

Chandler Owen was drafted into the army soon after he returned to New York. He was sent to a training camp in the South. Randolph received his draft notice in October 1918, but the war ended before he was called to active duty. Randolph swore he would have gone to jail rather than fight in a war he opposed.

The African Americans who did fight in Europe came home to cheering and parades. About one million New Yorkers turned out to watch the 369th Infantry march along Fifth Avenue from the southern tip of Manhattan all the way to Harlem.

Many African Americans expected better treatment from whites after displaying heroism in the war. What they got instead was violence. Whites sought to prevent blacks from moving into their neighborhoods or competing against them for jobs. More than seventy African Americans were lynched in the year after the peace treaty. Some died wearing their World War I uniforms.

Race riots erupted in at least twenty-five cities and towns between January and December 1919. For three days in Washington, D.C., during the bloody "Red Summer" of that year, mobs of white veterans moved through the city destroying blacks' homes. The rioting in Chicago left more than one thousand families homeless and 537 people injured. Thirty-eight people—blacks and whites—were killed.

New Yorkers turn out to cheer the 369th Infantry, known as the "Harlem Hell-Fighters," as they parade up Fifth Avenue following victory in World War I.

The editors of the *Messenger* inspired their readers to stand up against white mobs. They published the stirring poem "If We Must Die," by the African-American writer Claude McKay.

If We Must Die

If we must die, let it not be like hogs
　　Hunted and penned in an inglorious spot,
While round us bark the mad and hungry dogs,
　　Making their mock at our accursed lot.
If we must die, oh, let us nobly die,
　　So that our precious blood may not be shed
In vain; then even the monsters we defy
　　Shall be constrained to honor us, though dead!
Oh, kinsmen! We must meet the common foe;
　　Though far outnumbered, let us still be brave.
And for their thousand blows deal one death-blow!
　　What though before us lies the open grave?
Like men we'll face the murderous, cowardly pack,
Pressed to the wall, dying, but—fighting back![6]

The *Messenger* also printed a cartoon that was unsettling to the white population. It showed a heavily armed black man, the "New Negro," shooting into a crowd of whites. "Since the government won't stop mob violence," says the man in the cartoon, "I'll take a hand."[7] Items such as these prompted a Justice Department official to call the *Messenger* "the most dangerous of all the Negro publications."[8]

An African-American family's possessions lie strewn across the lawn after whites destroyed their home in the riots of 1919.

Randolph and Owen were becoming well-known figures in the world of liberal politics. They were invited to lecture at New York's Rand School of Social Science, which had been founded by the American Socialist Society to educate working people. Many leading socialist and liberal thinkers taught at the Rand School. They included Norman Thomas, who would head the Socialist Party following the death of Eugene Debs in 1926.

Meanwhile, the men and women of Harlem were listening to a new messenger of hope. He was Marcus

Garvey, the Jamaican-born leader of the Universal Negro Improvement Association (UNIA). Garvey talked about "a new world of black men . . . a nation of sturdy men making their impress upon civilization and causing a new light to dawn upon the human race."[9] He told African Americans to take pride in their dark skin. He called for people of African descent to band together to raise themselves economically and to forget about gaining acceptance from whites. He also spoke of bringing black Americans to Africa to create a country of their own. The UNIA formed the Black Star Steamship Line to transport people and goods to Africa.

At first Randolph welcomed Garvey and worked with him. But he soon came to see that Garvey was peddling dreams. Randolph said it was unlikely that African Americans could colonize Africa, a continent controlled by European powers. Also, ventures such as the Black Star Steamship Line wasted African Americans' money.

Garvey was harmful, Randolph said, because he failed to address African Americans' biggest problems, such as segregation, lynching, and denial of the right to vote. Randolph wrote that "instead of achieving its goal, that is, making the Negro 'First,' [the UNIA] actually results in achieving just the opposite, that is, making the Negro 'last.'"[10] Randolph and Owen popularized the slogan "Garvey Must Go!"[11]

In its own publication, the *Negro World*, the UNIA promised to get even with its critics. Randolph's life was threatened more than once. On September 5, 1922, he received a sinister warning—a package containing a severed human hand. It was impossible to prove who sent the menacing parcel, but Randolph was sure that it came from Garvey's supporters. Garvey, though, claimed to know nothing about it.

No harm came to Randolph, however. Garvey's influence declined rapidly after he was arrested in 1923 for illegal use of the U.S. mail. He was sentenced to prison and later ordered to leave the United States.

Although Randolph always spoke his mind, he rarely engaged in feuds. More often, he brought people together to solve problems or share ideas. In 1917, he had briefly organized a union of elevator operators in New York City. In 1920, he and Owen had formed the Friends of Negro Freedom, a discussion group. The members met at Randolph's apartment on Sunday mornings for breakfast and spirited talk. They arranged for Norman Thomas and other Socialists to speak in Harlem. In 1922, Asa Randolph's brother, James, joined the group. James had moved to New York to study at City College and was living with Asa and Lucille.

The 1920s brought change and loss to A. Philip Randolph. In 1923, Chandler Owen moved to Chicago to write editorials for an African-American newspaper.

Randolph now produced the *Messenger* with George Schuyler, a member of the Friends of Negro Freedom. In September 1924, Randolph's father, the Reverend Randolph, died in Jacksonville. A generation of African Americans who strove to better themselves in the aftermath of slavery was passing from the earth. Randolph wrote in the *Messenger,* "The death of such beautiful, rugged and stalwart, sacrificing characters is one of the tragedies of our period."[12] Elizabeth Randolph came to stay with her sons and daughter-in-law in the Harlem apartment.

The United States was at peace in the 1920s, and many people were optimistic. African-American thinkers talked less about politics and more about the arts. People were excited about the Harlem Renaissance, the flowering of African-American literature, art, and music that occurred between the two world wars.

Even though it featured more stories about books and painting, the *Messenger* was struggling to stay afloat. Fewer businesses paid to advertise in its pages. Lucille Randolph contributed less because her earnings had declined. Her husband's reputation as a radical had scared many customers away from her beauty shop.

But A. Philip Randolph's life was about to take a new direction. One morning in June 1925, a man stepped up to Randolph on a Harlem sidewalk and introduced himself. He was Ashley Totten, a Pullman porter and regular reader of the *Messenger*. Totten and some of his fellow porters wanted to start a union, but they needed help. Knowing of Randolph's interest in labor unions, he asked Randolph to meet with the men and tell them how to proceed. In Ashley Totten, Randolph observed more than a tall, well-dressed man with a West Indian accent. He spotted a quality he admired, which he called "a sort of fearlessness."[13] Randolph agreed to attend the meeting.

6

THE BROTHERHOOD IS BORN

Many Americans who traveled overnight by train in the first half of the twentieth century knew the friendly smile and helping hand of the Pullman porter. The porter worked for the Pullman Company, which owned and operated sleeping cars for train travel. He carried passengers' bags and helped people on and off the train. He made up their beds and polished their shoes while they slept. The porter responded to passengers' requests at any hour of the day or night.

Before meeting with the porters, Randolph researched their history and working conditions. He learned that George Pullman, who developed the sleeping car, hired newly freed slaves to be the first porters in 1867. In the years that followed, the majority of porters continued to be African American. They put in grueling hours. Although other railroad employees worked 240 hours per month, the porters were required to log 400 hours or 11,000 miles of travel, whichever they achieved first. The company expected them to be at the station several hours before departure to ready the sleeping cars and to assist passengers who were boarding. None of these hours counted toward the monthly total, though. The time clock ticked for the porters only when the trains were moving.

For all their hard work, the porters were poorly paid. In 1925, they earned $67.50 per month, on average, which was far less than other railroad workers were paid. From that small salary they had to buy their uniforms and the shoe polish that they used on the job. They had to pay for their meals and for lodging when they slept away from home between train trips. Porters depended on tips from passengers to support themselves and their families.

The Pullman Company got away with treating its workers so poorly because being a porter was the best job that many African Americans could get. Most African Americans in the South worked as tenant farmers. A tenant farmer plowed fields that belonged to someone else and gave part of the crop or the profit to the

A Pullman porter brings a glass of water to a passenger in a photograph from 1905. Porters performed this and similar duties in the 1920s.

filled the seats. Most were porters, but Randolph knew that some were spies sent by the Pullman Company to report on disloyal employees.

For that reason, Randolph instructed his audience to do nothing more than listen. Speaking up might put their jobs in danger. He gave the main speech, introduced guest speakers, and even sang the union song alone. Randolph said that the new union was to be called the Brotherhood of Sleeping Car Porters. He listed the union's demands: 240 hours of work per month, including time spent working while the trains stood in stations; and monthly wages of $150. The union was also demanding recognition as the porters' bargaining agent. This meant that union leaders would meet with the executives of the Pullman Company to discuss wages and other benefits. The union also would handle workers' grievances. The Brotherhood was insisting, too, that the company union—the Plan of Employee Representation—be abolished.

Because of the danger posed by spies, Randolph advised the porters to talk about the union only in private. Anyone who wanted to join could do so at the office of the *Messenger*, which was now the official publication of the Brotherhood of Sleeping Car Porters.

The next day, two hundred porters showed up to join the union. Within two months, half of the porters in New York were members. Those men were just a fraction of the ten thousand porters employed throughout the United States, though. To make the Brotherhood a national organization, one powerful enough to confront the mighty Pullman Company, Randolph needed to take his message on the road. He embarked on a tour of the United States and made sure that he visited cities where many porters lived. Ashley Totten, his chief assistant, was with him for much of the trip.

In Chicago, Randolph met Milton Webster, a large, plain-talking man. Webster had spent twenty years as a Pullman porter before being fired for trying to get the porters into a railroad workers' union. Webster's manner was brash, and he flatly rejected socialism. But he believed in the Brotherhood and knew how to get people together. Webster agreed to head the union's Chicago operation and became Randolph's trusted helpmate.

In St. Louis, Missouri, E. J. Bradley quit his job as a porter to work for the union, although the Brotherhood could not afford to pay him a regular salary. The trunk of his car became his office. In Oakland, California, Randolph enlisted the help of Morris "Dad" Moore, a retired porter. Moore talked up the union to porters coming into and out of Oakland.

This trip was the first of many that Randolph made to bring the union's message to the porters. He devoted great energy to the task and often traveled with

An early photograph of the officials of the Brotherhood of Sleeping Car Porters. Front row, left to right: C. L. Dellums, Bennie Smith of Detroit, Milton Webster, A. Philip Randolph, Ashley Totten, and R. J. Bradley of St. Louis.

almost no money in his pocket. The porters in one city sometimes took up a collection to pay his train fare to the next place. Traveling forced him to give up time with his family. Many times, he and Lucille were apart on their shared birthday or on their anniversary. In March 1926, when Randolph's mother died in New York, he was in California and could not afford to go home for her funeral. But all the hard work had its rewards. By December 1925, the Brotherhood of Sleeping Car Porters had fifty-seven hundred members.

(This total included a small number of maids.) By late 1926, the union had offices in sixteen cities. It was a union "of Negroes by Negroes for Negroes," Randolph said.[3]

The Pullman Company had easily crushed the earlier porters' unions, and it now set out to destroy the Brotherhood of Sleeping Car Porters. Hundreds of porters who belonged to the Brotherhood lost their jobs. Thirty porters in St. Louis were fired in one dismal day. The company even took away Dad Moore's pension. Needing to protect their livelihood, many porters kept their membership in the Brotherhood secret. They paid their dues but stayed away from union meetings. They avoided being seen with Randolph.

Pullman Company executives vowed never to negotiate with A. Philip Randolph. They spread a rumor that he was a Communist and a troublemaker. They tried—without success—to have him picked up by the police. Randolph had committed no crime, but the company wanted to take a picture of him behind bars and show it to the porters.

Many African Americans worried that Randolph's efforts would worsen conditions for the porters. The NAACP, the National Urban League, the African-American press, and many African-American preachers supported the position of the Pullman Company. They warned that Randolph was too radical, or that he was interested only in making a profit.

Randolph defended himself to the porters. "When I enlisted in the cause I knew that slander would attempt to blacken my character," he said. "But I am undaunted and unafraid. The only reward I seek is that your cause secures a full and complete vindication."[4] He told Milton Webster, "We haven't the money the Pullman Company has, but what we lack in money . . . we should make up in spirit and the will to conquer. . . . nothing under the sun can halt the onward, conquering march of the iron battalions of the Brotherhood of Sleeping Car Porters."[5]

Success appeared close at hand in May 1926, when Congress passed the Railway Labor Act. This federal law created the Board of Mediation to settle labor disputes that threatened to disrupt the nation's rail service. Because trains carried nearly all goods and passengers at that time, the government wanted to keep them running on schedule.

Randolph viewed the new law as a tool for forcing the Pullman Company into talks. Acting in accordance with the law, he notified the Pullman Company that the Brotherhood represented a majority of the porters—53 percent—and he requested a meeting. "For once black men are seriously preparing to write their own economic contracts which will benefit their children and their children's children," he said.[6] When the company failed to respond to his letter, he wrote again. When the Pullman Company continued to ignore him, Randolph turned to the Board of Mediation for help. The board appointed Edward P. Morrow, a former governor of Kentucky, to look into the matter.

But even Morrow bowed before the Pullman Company. When company leaders told him that 85 percent of the porters belonged to the Plan of Employee Representation, he saw no need to check out the truth of their claim or the nature of the plan. Randolph supplied written testimony from porters who had been forced to join the company union, but even that made no difference. The Pullman Company said that the porters already had a union and refused to meet with the Brotherhood. Morrow believed the company and closed his investigation.

Vowing that "a quitter never wins and a winner never quits," Randolph kept fighting.[7] He knew that in the case of an emergency, the Board of Mediation could force the Pullman Company into meetings. One way for the porters to create an emergency was to go on strike. If every porter in the Brotherhood walked off the job, the company would be forced to listen. In May 1928, more than half of the 10,994 porters voted to take part in a strike if Randolph called for one. To Randolph, the strike vote was "a sign of the iron resolution of the men to fight to the finish for their rights."[8] He announced that the strike would begin on June 28, 1928.

7

VICTORY

June 28, 1928, came and went without a strike. Randolph had weighed his goals for the union against the day-to-day needs of the porters, and the porters had won. At that time, the union was too little and too poor to hold a strike and succeed. Randolph knew that if the strike failed, many of those who took part would be fired. He also knew that strikes often led to violence. Randolph could not ask the union members to risk their jobs or their safety, so he called off the strike. Convinced that no emergency existed, the Board of Mediation closed its investigation.

The Pullman Company granted a small pay raise to the porters and maids to weaken their resolve to strike in the future. The company hired several Filipino workers to show the African Americans that they could easily be replaced. Also, company officials made it known that they might bargain with the union if Randolph resigned as president. But Randolph suspected that they were bluffing, and he refused to resign.

The year 1928 was a gloomy one for A. Philip Randolph. He had spent nearly three years building the Brotherhood of Sleeping Car Porters but had failed to make the Pullman Company listen to the union's demands. And in January, his brother, James, had died of diphtheria. At the time of his death, James Randolph had nearly finished his studies at City College and was preparing to enter the University of Berlin. A. Philip Randolph said that losing James was the saddest event in his life. "I cannot bear to live in a world without my brother," he told a friend.[1] But Randolph's life and his work went on.

In 1929, when the Brotherhood of Sleeping Car Porters held a national convention in Chicago, Randolph was reelected president and Milton Webster was elected vice president. Many porters had lost faith in the union, though. Membership had dropped, and the treasury was nearly empty. The *Messenger* had ceased publication in 1928. Some people said that only one person, A. Philip Randolph, believed that the Brotherhood had a future. Unwilling to see his union collapse, Randolph applied for membership in the American Federation of Labor (AFL).

Founded in 1886, the AFL was an alliance of independent labor unions that found strength in numbers. AFL unions supported one another in disputes with management, and they aided workers who wanted to form unions. They also lobbied Congress for laws to protect the interests of workers.

The history of organized labor in the United States was a story of strife and violence. Some companies had resorted to threats, beatings, and gunfire to maintain control over wages and working conditions. Many striking laborers had been injured or killed fighting for dignity on the job.

In 1894, the Pullman Company had been at the center of one of the largest strikes in U.S. history. In June of that year, three thousand people who built sleeping cars in the company's Chicago plant walked off the job. The reasons for the strike included cuts in wages and the firing of workers who were on a bargaining committee.

The protest spread, and by July, 125,000 workers employed by twenty different railroads were involved. U.S. Army units went to Chicago to prevent violence, but at least thirty protesters died in clashes with the soldiers. The strike lasted into September. By that time, the workers were growing desperate for money. They drifted back to work, and the strike ended.

Randolph sought membership in the AFL despite the fact that most unions refused to admit African Americans. Some unions had clauses in their constitutions that limited membership to whites. Others permitted blacks to join separate, segregated units. There were exceptions, of course. The United Mine Workers and the International Ladies Garment Workers Union were two large, influential unions that freely admitted members of all races. Officially, the AFL barred from membership any union that excluded African Americans, but the rule was rarely enforced.

Some African Americans criticized the Brotherhood for allying itself with a racist organization. They pointed out that Randolph himself had attacked the AFL, calling it the "American Separation of Labor."[2] Milton Webster answered the critics matter-of-factly, saying, "In America, if we should stay out of everything that's prejudiced we wouldn't be in anything."[3]

Randolph viewed entry into the AFL as a step toward integrating all of organized labor and improving conditions for all workers. He stressed that black and white laborers would have greater bargaining power if they were united. "The labor movement cannot afford to be split along any lines," he said.[4]

As the 1930s began, blacks and whites alike found

themselves out of work. Labor unions throughout the nation were losing members. Five million workers belonged to AFL unions in 1918. By 1933, union membership had dropped to 2.5 million, or just over 4 percent of the workforce. The United States had entered the Great Depression, a decade of severe financial hardship.

"The depression brought everybody down a peg or two. And the Negro had but few pegs to fall," said the poet Langston Hughes.[5] African Americans were the first to be fired as stores and factories closed. They often saw their jobs given to whites who needed work. Joblessness had always affected a higher percentage of blacks than whites in the United States. During the depression, the gap widened. In 106 cities surveyed by the National Urban League in 1931, unemployment was 30 percent to 60 percent greater among blacks than among whites.

Community relief programs tended to overlook the needs of African Americans. Many charity soup kitchens served only whites. In Jacksonville, Florida, Randolph's hometown, blacks hired to work on relief projects were paid 20 cents an hour. Whites working beside them received 30 cents an hour. Work-relief programs in other cities also paid blacks less than whites.

The depression dealt a serious blow to the Brotherhood of Sleeping Car Porters. The union lost nine-tenths of its members. With its money dwindling, the Brotherhood was evicted from its New York office. Randolph earned ten dollars a week from the union, and after Lucille Randolph's beauty shop went out of business, the couple lived on his meager salary. There was no money to buy clothes, so Randolph conducted the union's business wearing frayed shirts and worn-out suits. Although his appearance made some of the porters feel ashamed, Randolph ignored the condition of his wardrobe. He managed to be as dignified in rags as he was in fine attire.

Fiorello La Guardia, the mayor of New York City, offered Randolph a job with the city government. B. F. McLaurin of the Brotherhood's New York office heard La Guardia say, "Phil, you have holes in your shoes. It will take a lifetime to organize the porters. Take a job with the city. You need to eat and pay your rent."[6] Randolph, unwilling to admit defeat, turned down La Guardia's offer.

In 1932, Americans elected Franklin Delano Roosevelt president of the United States. Roosevelt promised the nation a "New Deal," a series of programs to revive the economy and get people working. The president and his advisers believed that strong labor unions would help the economy start growing again. One key piece of New Deal legislation, the National Industrial Recovery Act, guaranteed workers the right to organize and bargain collectively with their employers. Workers now had the right to choose their own representatives. Another new law, the Emergency Railroad Transportation Act, outlawed company unions in the railroad industry.

Working men and women no longer feared that union membership might cost them badly needed jobs. They returned to their unions in large numbers. Porters and maids rejoined the Brotherhood, confident that with federal laws backing him up, Randolph would now force the Pullman Company to cooperate.

New Deal programs created jobs for millions of Americans, black and white. This young woman in Howard, Virginia, was employed to draft maps by the National Youth Administration, an agency that hired teenagers and young adults.

Randolph wrote to the managers of the Pullman Company again, but they still ignored his letters. When he sought to find out why, he received a rude shock. The government had classified the Pullman Company as a hotel service rather than as a railroad firm. The new law applied only to certain industries, and the hotel business was not one of them. Even the government of the United States had let the porters down.

Most people would have given up in the face of such obstacles, but Randolph kept trying. He turned for help to Senator Clarence Dill of Washington State, a longtime friend of the porters' union. In the summer of 1934, Dill managed to have the Pullman Company reclassified as a railroading firm. But even then the company refused to meet with the union. Brazenly defying the law, the Pullman Company laid off hundreds of porters who favored the union, whether or not they were known to be members.

The company also asked several trusted employees to start a new union, the Pullman Porters Protective Association. Company executives claimed that it was an independent union because the members paid dues. But in truth the company controlled the Protective Association.

Once more, Randolph turned to the Board of Mediation. He asked the board to order an election so that the porters and maids could vote to decide which union would represent them. The Board of Mediation supervised a secret-ballot election on June 25, 1935. The Brotherhood beat the Protective Association by a huge majority.

On July 29, 1935, Randolph and the other leaders of the Brotherhood sat down as equals with company executives at the Pullman Company offices in Chicago. They began two years of negotiations. On August 25, 1937, exactly twelve years after the Brotherhood was formed, the company and the union signed an agreement. It gave the porters the largest pay raise that they had ever received. The agreement set minimum monthly pay at $89.50 and reduced the work month to 240 hours.

Said C. L. Dellums, who succeeded Dad Moore in Oakland, "We were a handful of Negroes. Had nothing: no money, no experience in this. I used to say that all we had was what God gave the lizard."[7] Yet guided by A. Philip Randolph, these African-American union leaders had forced a large corporation to meet their demands. Dellums explained what the hard-won victory meant to all African Americans: "That was the first economic agreement that was ever signed in this country by Negroes with a white institution. . . . That was a tremendous thing. It was a great inspirational thing to the entire race."[8]

8

THE WILL TO STRUGGLE

Through his long contest with the Pullman Company, A. Philip Randolph became a leader in the labor movement and in the African-American community. People called him "St. Philip of the Pullman Porters,"[1] or "Mr. Black Labor."[2]

In February 1936, Randolph was elected president of a new organization, the National Negro Congress (NNC). The congress enabled African Americans from all over the country to join forces to combat the economic, social, and political problems of the depression. Randolph expected the NNC to be a "cementing force" that would hold people together.[3]

Randolph resigned from the NNC four years later, after discovering that many Communists were among its members. Communists looked upon the fight for racial equality as part of a larger conflict between the poorer classes and the capitalists. Like Socialists, they believed that workers should own factories, mines, and railroads. Communism was more extreme than socialism, though. When put into practice, it stripped citizens of basic rights. In the Communist-run Soviet Union, people were denied freedom of speech, freedom of the press, and the right to vote. Randolph suspected that the Communists within the NNC cared more about aiding the Soviet Union than helping African Americans gain their civil rights.

Randolph continued to push to end segregation within the American Federation of Labor. Year after year, he urged the AFL to organize African-American workers. He argued that bringing African Americans into the nation's unions would increase labor's bargaining power with employers. Yet most white unionists refused to listen. They feared that admitting blacks as equals would make the jobs of white workers less secure.

The first unions in the AFL had been composed of skilled artisans. That is, there were separate unions of plumbers, bricklayers, machinists, and other kinds of workers who had mastered the skills of their trades. Unions of this type had no place for the millions of unskilled workers who toiled in the nation's factories. For this reason, some labor leaders wanted to organize workers in a different way. They favored a single union for all the workers in each industry, skilled tradespeople and unskilled laborers alike.

In 1935, John L. Lewis of the United Mine Workers formed a committee within the AFL to organize workers by industry. Lewis's group was known as the Committee for Industrial Organization (CIO). In 1936 and 1937, the CIO led dramatic strikes that shut down some of the nation's largest automobile and steel plants. The strikes brought many unskilled workers into industrial unions.

The unions of skilled trades objected strongly to the policies of the CIO, however. In 1937, the AFL expelled the unions belonging to the CIO. In 1938, these thirty-two unions formed a new alliance, the Congress of Industrial Organizations, which was also called the CIO.

Because most African Americans in heavy industry held jobs requiring a low level of skill, many found a welcome in the CIO. John L. Lewis appealed to Randolph to bring the Brotherhood of Sleeping Car Porters into the new organization. But since the CIO was already admitting African Americans, it did not need A. Philip Randolph's help. He chose to keep the Brotherhood in the AFL so that he could keep working to integrate its unions. "My fight, the fight to organize

Negro workers, is in the AFL. I must stay here and carry on that fight," he said.[4]

World events were about to draw Randolph into another fight for fair treatment. In 1933, Adolf Hitler's Nazi Party had come to power in Germany. The Nazis considered Aryans—people of Northern European heritage—to be a superior group, or "master race." They persecuted Jews and other minority groups within Germany's borders. Over the next few years, the Nazi forces gained strength. Germany occupied Austria and part of Czechoslovakia in 1938. After Nazi forces invaded Poland in 1939, Great Britain and France declared war on Germany.

A major war erupted in Europe for the second time in Randolph's life. He was ready now to support the war effort if the United States became involved. As a member of the nation's largest minority group, one that had spent generations in slavery, Randolph understood that racial and ethnic hatred had to be combated wherever it appeared.

There was only one way for African Americans to serve their country, Randolph said, and that was on an equal basis with whites. He took aim at two targets: the discrimination in the defense industries and the segregation that still existed in U.S. military service.

By 1940, the United States was sending weapons to Great Britain. American factories were halting the production of consumer goods and gearing up to make airplanes, tanks, and guns for future use. Thousands of people who had been unemployed during the Great Depression found steady jobs in defense plants—if they were white.

Although there was a shortage of workers, companies involved in defense production refused to hire blacks to perform skilled labor. In some cities, manufacturers brought in white workers from rural areas rather than employ the black men and women who lived nearby.

"Negroes will be considered only as janitors and in other similar capacities," said the president of North American Aviation, a defense manufacturer.[5] "Under no circumstances would Negroes be employed as aircraft workers or mechanics in the plant," he continued.[6] The federal government was doing nothing to ensure equal employment. In fact, government-sponsored defense-training programs were teaching only whites.

In September 1940, Randolph went to Washington, D.C., with Walter F. White of the NAACP and T. Arnold Hill of the National Urban League to discuss this situation with President Roosevelt. The president made small talk and promised to look into unfair hiring practices. Two weeks later, Randolph was stunned to hear the president's secretary announce that the African-American leaders had approved the government's policy of segregation!

Randolph became convinced that he would have to

Famed African-American photographer Gordon Parks took this picture of Randolph in 1942.

force employers and the government to change their ways. Strikes and picket lines—the weapons of organized labor—had taught him that "nothing stirs and shapes public sentiment like physical action."[7] To win the right to serve their country, African Americans needed to take action in a big way, to make President Roosevelt and the Congress sit up and take notice.

On a railroad journey through the South, passing the homes of poor African Americans, Randolph came up with a bold plan. He told Milton Webster, who sat beside him, "I think we ought to get 10,000 Negroes and march down Pennsylvania Avenue [in Washington, D.C.] asking for jobs in defense plants and integration of the armed forces."[8]

"Here it comes again," Webster thought.[9] It seemed to him that "Brother Randolph was always figuring out something for us to do, sticking his nose in everything to see where he can stir something up."[10] Randolph said he was sure that his plan "would wake up and shock official Washington as it has never been shocked before."[11]

Wherever he presented his idea—in Savannah, Jacksonville, Harlem, or Chicago—African Americans responded to news of the march with enthusiasm. Interest was so strong that Randolph now said that he would bring one hundred thousand people to Washington. "Let the Negro masses speak!" he proclaimed.[12] Randolph warned African Americans that they faced a "tremendous and difficult" task.[13] Achieving success "will require sacrifice. It will tax the Negroes' courage, determination and will to struggle."[14] He reminded audiences that "the Negroes' stake in national defense is big. It consists of jobs, thousands of jobs. It may represent millions, yes, hundreds of millions of dollars in wages. It consists of new industrial opportunities and hope. This is worth fighting for."[15]

Randolph brought together ministers, union leaders, and other distinguished African Americans to form the March on Washington Committee, the group that would coordinate the event. The march was scheduled for July 1, 1941.

The nation's capital was a segregated city in 1941. African Americans traveling by bus or rail from the North to the South had to transfer to separate "Jim Crow" seating when they reached Washington, D.C. Laws barred African Americans from eating in restaurants or sleeping in hotels in downtown Washington. Some hospitals in the District of Columbia admitted white patients only, while others set aside certain wards for the treatment of blacks. Most of the African Americans who lived in Washington occupied run-down housing and sent their children to crowded, inferior schools.

Roosevelt's advisers warned him that the arrival of one hundred thousand African-American marchers needing food and shelter would strain the resources of this racially divided city. Some predicted that violence would result. They asked, how would the world respond to the sight of whites fighting blacks in the capital of the United States?

The president asked Mayor La Guardia and the first lady, Eleanor Roosevelt, to meet with Randolph and persuade him to call off the march. Eleanor Roosevelt had always championed racial equality, but even she agreed that this march was a bad idea. She reminded Randolph that if rioting broke out, the African-American cause would be harmed rather than helped. Randolph listened, but his mind was made up.

On June 18, 1941, President Roosevelt invited Randolph and Walter White to the White House. "Phil," the president pleaded, "you can't bring 100,000 Negroes to Washington. We can't have that."[16] Although Randolph secretly doubted that one hundred thousand people would actually show up, he assured Roosevelt that the protest would go ahead as planned. Roosevelt then promised the two men that he would demand better treatment of African-American workers if they would call off the march. But the word of the president of the United States was not good enough for A. Philip Randolph. He needed to see something in writing.

On June 25, 1941, six days before the scheduled march, Roosevelt signed Executive Order 8802. This document required the federal government and companies with defense contracts to hire workers without regard to race, religion, or national origin. Roosevelt established the Fair Employment Practices Committee (later called the Fair Employment Practices Commission) to investigate complaints. Randolph called the executive order "the most significant and meaningful U.S. government declaration affecting Negroes since the Emancipation Proclamation."[17]

The president's order failed to integrate the armed forces, but Randolph felt satisfied enough to call off the march. With the United States on the verge of war, a continued protest could make African Americans hostile toward the military in a time of national crisis. His decision disappointed many people who had looked forward to the march.

For a time, all of black America had pulled together to make something happen. To capture that energy, Randolph organized the March on Washington Movement, which would promote nonviolent protest. Randolph predicted that peaceful demonstrations would one day end Jim Crow segregation in the South. The March on Washington Movement remained active through the late 1940s.

The United States entered World War II in December 1941, after Japanese planes attacked the American naval base at Pearl Harbor, Hawaii. Approximately 1 million African Americans fought

A military officer asks about train schedules at Washington, D.C.'s Union Station in 1942. He was among the 1 million African Americans who served their country in World War II.

overseas in the army, navy, or marines. America's black fighting men and women achieved some important gains. For example, African Americans first served as military pilots during World War II.

The Fair Employment Practices Commission looked into numerous reports of discrimination in hiring, but it was not a perfect agency. It had too few people and too little money to investigate every complaint. Also, it had no power to enforce the president's order.

Racial bias continued to affect defense employment,

although to a lesser degree than before the war. By 1944, 8.3 percent of the defense-industry workforce was African American. Many African Americans were also added to the government payroll. Thanks to A. Philip Randolph's will to struggle, the U.S. government had taken measures to integrate the workplace for the first time.

9

LABOR'S CONSCIENCE

The postwar years were a time of peace and plenty in the United States. Factories again produced goods for the buying public. Returning soldiers married, started families, and settled into jobs.

African Americans had a tougher time earning a living than whites did, though. A 1947 government report stated that minority workers often earned less than whites doing the same kind of work. They also received fewer promotions than whites did. This kind of discrimination occurred in private business and government alike.

African Americans were pressing for greater equality in many facets of American life. In 1946, the Supreme Court banned segregation on buses traveling between states. A new organization, the Congress of Racial Equality (CORE), began the long process of making southern states obey that ruling. In April 1947, CORE sent sixteen men—eight blacks and eight whites—on the Journey of Reconciliation. The men spent three weeks riding public buses through the South and defying the practice of segregated seating. They were taking a real risk. At least six African Americans had been lynched in 1946, and twenty-two attempted lynchings had been prevented. The riders were fairly lucky. Although one was punched and four were arrested, they returned safely from their mission.

Randolph, meanwhile, was working to integrate the armed forces. In 1947, when President Harry S. Truman called for a peacetime draft, Randolph knew that it was time to take action. He helped to form yet another organization, the League for Nonviolent Civil Disobedience Against Military Segregation. (People practicing *civil disobedience* refuse to obey a law that they believe is unjust. They view their actions as a peaceful form of protest.)

One of the hardest workers in the league was its executive secretary, Bayard Rustin. The thirty-eight-year-old Rustin was a controversial figure who had been involved with communism in the 1930s. A pacifist, he

The March on Washington Movement operated stores that sold books and cards. The money raised was used to support nonviolent demonstrations for social justice.

had spent twenty-eight months in prison rather than fight in World War II. Rustin also had planned the Journey of Reconciliation and was one of the riders arrested.

Rustin never forgot Randolph's kindness during their first meeting. When Rustin entered Randolph's office, the older man "stood up, came out from behind his desk, met me in the middle of the room, shook hands, offered me a seat—and I was nothing but a nobody."[1] Randolph asked many questions about Rustin's ideas but talked little about himself.

Responding to the draft call, Randolph announced that his new group was seeking another executive order, one that would integrate the armed services. At a White House meeting on March 22, 1948, he hinted at what his followers might do to achieve desegregation. "Mr. President," he said, "the mood among Negroes of this country is that they will never bear arms again until all forms of bias and discrimination are abolished."[2] This was a serious threat. Anyone who refused to serve in the military would be breaking a federal law.

President Truman, angered by such frank talk, replied, "I wish you hadn't made that statement. I don't like it at all."[3] He declined to issue an executive order.

On March 31, Randolph repeated his warning. He told the Senate Armed Services Committee that if segregation continued in the armed forces, millions of African Americans would refuse to serve. "Negroes will not take a jim crow draft lying down," he said. "The conscience of the world will be shaken as by nothing else when thousands and thousands of us second-class Americans choose imprisonment in preference to permanent military slavery."[4]

Lucille Randolph read her husband's statement in a newspaper and sent him a telegram of support. "Your remarks yesterday before Senate committee [make] me very proud," she wrote.[5]

Back in New York, Randolph again gave speeches on Harlem street corners. He implored African Americans not to join a fighting force that segregated them because of their race.

African Americans were divided in their support of Randolph. To many people, someone who refused to serve his or her country—for any reason—was a traitor. But one prominent African American who sided with Randolph was Congressman Adam Clayton Powell of New York. Powell reminded people that the whites who created the segregated military system were "traitors to our Constitution and to our Bill of Rights."[6] Most members of the group that would be drafted, young black men, favored the protest.

In July 1948, Randolph took his fight to Philadelphia, Pennsylvania. The Democratic National Party was holding its convention there to nominate Truman for the fall presidential election. Fearing that the army of picketers outside the convention hall would turn African-American voters against him, Truman issued two executive orders. The first one called for the armed forces to integrate "as rapidly as possible."[7] In this document, the president decreed that every American in uniform deserved "equality of treatment and opportunity regardless of race, color, religion, or national origin."[8] The second executive order established the Fair Employment Board to end discrimination in federal agencies. (The Fair

Employment Practices Commission, formed during the Roosevelt administration, had been dissolved in 1946.)

Integrated military units saw combat for the first time in the Korean War, which began in June 1950. By the time the war ended in July 1953, more than 90 percent of African-American soldiers were serving in racially mixed units.

Randolph decided to disband the League for Nonviolent Civil Disobedience in August 1948, after its goal was achieved. Some of the group's younger members, including Bayard Rustin, kept it going for a few months, though. They even held a press conference and criticized Randolph for giving up. Rustin soon felt ashamed of his actions and avoided Randolph for two years. When he at last saw Randolph again, he received a warm greeting. Randolph asked him, "Where have you been? You *know* I've needed you."[9]

Rustin commented, "Such character! He never said a word about what I had done to him."[10]

In 1950, the eighteen thousand members of the porters' union reelected Randolph as their president. Five years later, he took on a larger role in organized labor.

In 1955, the American Federation of Labor and the Congress of Industrial Organizations united to create a single alliance, the AFL-CIO. The issue that had divided them, whether to form trade or industrial unions, no longer seemed to matter very much. The merger

Randolph, in the front row, represented the AFL (American Federation of Labor) at an international trade union conference in Milan, Italy, in 1951.

would give organized labor greater power. It would permit unions to "make a better and more vital contribution to the community as a whole and to the welfare and security of our nation," said AFL-CIO president George Meany.[11] Meany was a former plumber who had earned his position through years of hard work on behalf of U.S. laborers.

The AFL-CIO constitution stated that "all workers whatever their race, color, creed, or national origin are entitled to share in the full benefits of trade union organization."[12] As a sign of this new commitment to equality, Randolph and another African-American union president, Willard Townsend of the United Transport Service Employees, were appointed to the AFL-CIO's executive council. Randolph also served on a committee that investigated bias in labor unions. In 1957, he became a vice president of the AFL-CIO.

Randolph expected nothing less than strict enforcement of the new constitution. His views brought him into conflict with Meany, who wanted to rid labor unions of racism gradually. Time and again, Randolph rose in AFL-CIO meetings to protest because unions that excluded African Americans were being allowed to remain in the federation. Other delegates complained that he was acting as the "conscience" of the AFL-CIO.[13] Many of them, weary of his speeches, left the room as soon as he started to speak.

But Randolph persisted. At the 1959 AFL-CIO convention, he brought up the topic of race so many times that George Meany lost his temper. First, Randolph objected when members wanted to readmit the International Longshoremen's Association (ILA). This union had been expelled from the AFL-CIO for corruption. Randolph pointed out that although the ILA had rid itself of crooked officials, it discriminated against African Americans and Puerto Ricans. The AFL-CIO voted to readmit the ILA anyway.

Next, Randolph demanded that two unions be

expelled because their constitutions barred African Americans from membership. Later in the day, he spoke out against unions that admitted African Americans to separate local chapters. Following this final interruption of business, an enraged Meany shouted, "Just who elected you, Phil, to represent all the American Negroes?"[14]

Randolph had survived many years of labor struggles and had stood up to two U.S. presidents. It would take more than yelling to make him give up. Unbending but always polite, Randolph said afterward, "I know George didn't mean it. When he thinks it over, he'll regret it."[15] Randolph formed the Negro American Labor Council (NALC) to increase the presence of African Americans in unions. He served as NALC president from 1960 until 1966. And he continued to prod George Meany.

Meany complained that Randolph was acting unfairly. It seemed to him that instead of working with the other union leaders to help African Americans, Randolph was creating disturbances and making the AFL-CIO look bad. In 1961, the executive council voted to censure Randolph. (Censure is an expression of strong disapproval.) Meany used this occasion to clarify his reasons for tolerating racism. He explained that expelling a union from the AFL-CIO did nothing to stop it from discriminating. In fact, once an offending union was out of the organization, it was free to become even more racist. Education and persuasion within the AFL-CIO were much better weapons than expulsion, Meany contended.

But Meany soon took a stronger stand against racial bias in organized labor. He barred unions in the AFL-CIO from holding meetings in segregated restaurants and hotels. He added members to the civil rights committee, and he sought advice from Whitney M. Young, Jr., of the National Urban League. Meany took these steps because the nation's attitude toward civil rights was changing. Americans of all races were growing less tolerant of discrimination.

In 1954, the U.S. Supreme Court had ruled that segregated public schools violated the rights of African-American children. In so doing, the Court reversed its 1896 ruling allowing facilities that were "separate but equal." In December 1955, the African Americans of Montgomery, Alabama, began a 381-day boycott of their city's buses. Led by the Reverend Martin Luther King, Jr., they were protesting seating according to race. The Montgomery bus boycott resulted in another federal ruling, one that outlawed segregation in public transportation.

These court decisions failed to bring the opportunities for African Americans that many people desired. States and counties throughout the South quickly passed laws designed to prevent or delay school integration. Arkansas Governor Orville Faubus blocked the doorway to Central High School in Little Rock to keep African Americans from entering. In Montgomery, snipers shot at integrated buses moving along the streets, and terrorists bombed Dr. King's home.

Randolph held demonstrations to draw public attention to civil rights issues. In May 1957, he led the Prayer Pilgrimage in Washington, D.C. Twenty thousand people protested the violence that was occurring in the South and called for stronger civil rights laws.

On the speakers' platform at the Prayer Pilgrimage for Freedom, May 17, 1957, Randolph, center, chats with Roy Wilkins of the NAACP. To the right of Randolph are the Reverend Thomas Kilgore of the Friendship Baptist Church in New York City and the Reverend Martin Luther King, Jr.

On October 25, 1958, he was back in the nation's capital for the Youth March to Integrate Schools. Along with ten thousand young people, he walked along Constitution Avenue to the Lincoln Memorial. A second youth march was held on April 18, 1959. Randolph was traveling fifty thousand miles a year to lead marches, attend labor conferences, and give speeches.

A. Philip Randolph was sixty-nine years old, but he still had a great deal of work to do. Inequality was flourishing in America's offices and factories, and no one understood the needs of African-American workers better than he did. The facts were discouraging: Three-fourths of African-American workers held menial jobs, and more than half of all African Americans lived in poverty. Unemployment was twice as high among blacks as among whites. Many companies were moving their factories out of cities and into suburbs. As a result, thousands of African Americans living in inner-city neighborhoods lost their jobs because they lacked transportation to work.

Randolph still believed that good jobs and higher incomes would open up opportunities for his race. He was confident that he could help achieve those goals. He told an interviewer in 1958, "I am not an old man, my health is good and I have no intentions of retiring for some time."[16]

10

GENERATIONS

Although A. Philip Randolph remained vigorous and young in spirit, Lucille Randolph's health was failing. For years, painful arthritis had limited her movement. In the early 1950s, she fell and broke a hip, and she never fully recovered. She now spent her time confined to bed or a wheelchair. Randolph cooked for her whenever he was home, and he read to her in the evening. When he had to be away, a nurse took care of Lucille.

Lucille and A. Philip Randolph never had children. Over the years, they had built a life together and formed their own traditions. For instance, at Christmas they gave flowers and baskets of fruit to the other tenants in their apartment building. Lucille Randolph was "a beautiful and outgoing woman. She loved people," said B. F. McLaurin of the Brotherhood of Sleeping Car Porters. "She read a lot, [and] loved to tell stories. . . . She was also a woman of serious political ideas."[1]

Lucille Randolph died on April 12, 1963. Throughout his long career, Randolph had separated his personal and public lives. At age seventy-four, he was not about to change. He hid his sorrow even from the people closest to him and planned for a massive march on Washington. This time, it looked as though the great demonstration was going to take place.

Randolph conceived of this march as a way to bring together civil rights leaders, members of the clergy, and labor-union officials. The march would show that people throughout the nation, from every race and walk of life, favored equal opportunity for all. He feared that without a positive focus for their energy, protesters in some cities would turn to violence. "It became clear to him that unless there was a march on Washington that summer, there might be riots all over the country," said Bayard Rustin's secretary, Rachelle Horowitz.[2] Randolph also hoped to draw attention to the economic needs of African Americans.

Dr. Martin Luther King, Jr., had been thinking about holding a large protest march in Washington, too. When Randolph suggested that they plan a single demonstration, King agreed to cooperate. The nation's other African-American leaders consented to take part as well. "Neither Jim Farmer nor Roy Wilkins, nor Whitney Young, nor Dr. King would ignore a call from A. Philip Randolph," said Rachelle Horowitz.[3] (As it turned out, James Farmer was unable to attend the March on Washington because he was in jail in Louisiana, where he had been arrested for leading a demonstration.) Protestant, Catholic, and Jewish groups also asked to be part of the event.

As in the past, the idea of a mass gathering of African Americans in Washington, D.C., made politicians nervous. President John F. Kennedy, who had recently sent a civil rights bill to Congress, worried that if the marchers were unruly, his opponents in the House and Senate would vote against the proposed law. Like Franklin Roosevelt before him, Kennedy invited Randolph and the other march leaders to the White House and asked them to cancel their plans.

Randolph reminded President Kennedy that African Americans were staging angry protests in Birmingham and other American cities. "The Negroes are already in the streets," he said.[4] He explained that the civil rights movement was best led by people such as himself and Dr. King, who believed in peaceful civil disobedience. "The choice, Mr. President, is between a controlled and non-violent demonstration and an uncontrolled and violent one," Randolph stated.[5]

The leaders of the March on Washington meet with President John F. Kennedy and Vice President Lyndon Johnson at the White House.

Reluctantly, President Kennedy gave the march his backing.

Randolph had asked the AFL-CIO to endorse the march as well, but the executive council declined to do so. The council's concerns were the same as the president's. As George Meany phrased it, "I was fearful that there would be disorder, that people would get hurt, and that it would build up resentment in Congress."[6] The AFL-CIO permitted its member unions to take part in the march, though, and several planned to send representatives. Walter Reuther, president of the United Auto Workers, was one powerful labor leader who supported Randolph's effort. Reuther would march on behalf of organized labor.

It would be Bayard Rustin's job to get the thousands of people in and out of Washington as smoothly as possible. He would also see that they were fed and entertained, and make sure that toilets and first aid were available. Rustin worked closely with District of Columbia officials and the city police to ensure that the March on Washington was a peaceful, orderly event.

Thanks in large measure to Rustin's careful planning, the March on Washington is remembered as a bright moment in the civil rights struggle. It inspired millions of African Americans to take pride in their race. On the eve of the march, as people throughout the nation were packing their cars or boarding Washington-bound buses and trains, Randolph was already calling the event a success. "It has focused the attention of the country on the problems of human dignity and freedom for Negroes," he said. "It has reached the heart, mind, and conscience of America."[7]

Randolph had planned to lead the next day's march along Constitution Avenue toward the Lincoln Memorial, where the speeches were to be given. But when he and the other leaders left a premarch meeting at the White House, they saw that the people had started forward without them. Randolph and the others stepped into the moving river of people.

At the Lincoln Memorial, A. Philip Randolph, the grand old man of the civil rights movement, spoke about freedom and equality, as he had so often done in the past. He introduced the other speakers, including Dr. King. "When he introduced King, there were no dry eyes," said Timuel Black of the Negro American Labor Council. "Symbolically, it was like passing the torch from one generation of fighters to a new generation of fighters."[8]

King revealed the dream that dwelled in his heart, "a dream that one day this nation will rise up and live out the true meaning of its creed—we hold these truths to be self-evident that all men are created equal." It was a dream that "little black boys and black girls will be able to join hands with little white boys and white girls as sisters and brothers."[9] With that speech, King secured his place as an African-American leader of national importance.

The day was not free of dissent. George Lincoln Rockwell, head of the American Nazi Party, staged a small, competing demonstration near the Washington Monument. And Malcolm X, the charismatic spokesperson of the Nation of Islam, came to town to denounce the "Farce on Washington."[10] The Nation of Islam preached mistrust of whites and encouraged blacks to depend on themselves alone for advancement. At a press conference, Malcolm X criticized Randolph and his followers for begging favors from

Three weary march participants take a short break in Lafayette Park in view of the White House.

the "white man's Government."[11] But the few critical voices failed to dampen anyone's spirits.

After every speaker had been heard, the march leaders returned to the White House. President Kennedy praised King's speech and the dignity of the people who came to march. Then, Randolph pressured the president to toughen his civil rights bill, to add a section barring discrimination in employment. Randolph was most concerned about African-American teenagers. They often had trouble finding jobs and felt deeply discouraged. He explained that "they have no faith in anybody white. They have no faith in the Negro leadership. They have no faith in God. They have no faith in government. In other words, they believe the hand of society is against them."[12]

President Kennedy was assassinated in November 1963, before Congress passed his civil rights bill. In July 1964, President Lyndon B. Johnson signed into law the bill that Kennedy had drafted. This far-reaching Civil Rights Act made discrimination illegal in businesses serving the public, such as restaurants and hotels. As Randolph had requested, it outlawed racist decisions in hiring. In addition, it gave the attorney general power to protect citizens against discrimination.

The Voting Rights Act of 1965 protected the rights of all citizens to register to vote and take part in elections. Randolph viewed the new laws as progress. He said that the next challenge for the government and African Americans was to make sure the laws were enforced. "Whereas you may have a piece of legislation on the federal statute books, this does not mean that the country has accepted it," he noted.[13]

Increasingly, African-American leaders directed their efforts at the economic barriers to equality. For example, in 1966, Martin Luther King's organization, the Southern Christian Leadership Conference, demonstrated against inferior housing for African Americans in Chicago.

Many young people had lost patience with marches and sit-ins, though. They were demanding rapid social change. After Malcolm X was shot to death in Harlem in February 1965, other militants rose to prominence. In 1966, Huey Newton and Bobby Seale founded the Black Panther Party, a group that hoped to alter the structure of U.S. society. "We want land, bread, housing, education, clothing, justice, and peace," they stated.[14]

The same year, Stokely Carmichael of the Student Nonviolent Coordinating Committee summed up his belief in the strength and potential of African Americans by coining the term "Black Power." Black Power, he said, was "a call to reject the racist institutions of this society and its values."[15] Black power was about dignity, self-reliance, and people's right to use violence in self-defense.

Striking Memphis, Tennessee, sanitation workers demonstrate in 1968 under the menacing watch of the National Guard.

To Newton, Seale, Carmichael, and others of their generation, A. Philip Randolph's thinking was hopelessly old-fashioned.

Randolph objected to the militants' call for racial separation and to their acceptance of violence. But he understood their desire to make a difference, and he even felt a kinship with them. "I was a young black militant myself, the angry young man of my day," he said.[16] Randolph also understood that every generation owed a debt to the freedom fighters of earlier years. As he explained, "The black militants of today are standing on the shoulders of the 'new Negro radicals' of my day—the '20s, '30s and '40s. We stood upon

🔲🔲🔲🔲🔲🔲🔲🔲🔲🔲🔲🔲🔲🔲🔲🔲🔲🔲🔲🔲🔲🔲🔲🔲🔲🔲🔲🔲🔲🔲🔲🔲🔲🔲

the shoulders of the civil rights fighters of the Reconstruction era and they stood upon the shoulders of the black abolitionists."[17]

There were still many people who believed that peaceful protest and teamwork would never go out of style. In 1965, Randolph and Bayard Rustin formed an organization that would help younger generations continue Randolph's work. The A. Philip Randolph Institute was created to help labor unions and the African-American community work together. It was founded on the hope that cooperation might clear the way for racial and economic equality.

Throughout the 1960s, Randolph supported a variety of causes, such as voting rights and aid to the poor. He favored a guaranteed income for all Americans. He assisted striking workers, whether they were teachers in New York City, farm laborers in California, or sanitation workers in Memphis, Tennessee. He also spoke in favor of Israel. To Randolph, Jews and African Americans had something in common: Both groups had endured hatred and persecution. Randolph retired from the AFL-CIO and the Brotherhood of Sleeping Car Porters in April 1968.

The following April, he turned eighty. More than twelve hundred people gathered to honor him at the Waldorf Astoria Hotel in New York City. Randolph's friends and colleagues spoke about his influence and his accomplishments. George Meany saluted him as "a great trade unionist and a courageous fighter for justice and human decency."[18] Coretta Scott King thanked him for inspiring her late husband, Martin Luther King, Jr. She told those present that Randolph had provided Dr. King with "advice and counsel when he was a young man and a young leader."[19]

Randolph's friends had become his family, and Bayard Rustin looked after him like a devoted son.

At his eightieth birthday celebration, Randolph receives a standing ovation from the crowd and a warm greeting from Coretta Scott King. Bayard Rustin stands at the far left, beside AFL-CIO president George Meany. At the right, next to Randolph, is Governor Nelson Rockefeller of New York.

After Randolph was robbed outside his home in the summer of 1968, Rustin helped him move to an apartment in lower Manhattan near his own. The aged civil rights activist spent his last years living quietly there. He died on May 16, 1979, at age ninety.

In 1963, in his seventy-fourth year, Randolph had looked back, without regret, on the life he had led. He wrote, "If I were young again, I would not change the scheme of my life basically. In terms of the struggles and troubles incident to the type of life's work I have chosen, I would choose it again. . . ."[20]

CHRONOLOGY

1889—Asa Philip Randolph is born in Crescent City, Florida, on April 15.

1903—Attends the Cookman Institute and graduates
–1907　first in his class.

1911—Moves to Harlem in New York City.

1912—Enrolls in the City College of New York; becomes a Socialist.

1914—Marries Lucille Campbell Green; befriends Chandler Owen, a Columbia University student and fellow Socialist.

1917—Produces the *Hotel Messenger* with Owen; in November, founds the *Messenger* with Owen.

1918—Arrested in Cleveland, Ohio, for speaking against U.S. involvement in World War I.

1920—With Owen, forms the Friends of Negro Freedom.

1925—On August 25, becomes president of the Brotherhood of Sleeping Car Porters.

1928—The *Messenger* ceases publication.

1929—The Brotherhood joins the American Federation of Labor (AFL).

1935—In a government-supervised secret-ballot vote, the porters choose the Brotherhood to represent them; the union and the Pullman Company begin negotiations.

1936—Randolph is elected president of the National Negro Congress (NNC).

1937—On August 25, Pullman Company executives and union officials sign an agreement.

1940—Randolph resigns from the NNC because Communists have infiltrated the organization.

1941—Plans a July 1 march on Washington, D.C., to secure jobs in the defense industry for African Americans; cancels the march after President Franklin D. Roosevelt signs an executive order mandating equal employment in defense plants and federal jobs; forms the March on Washington Movement.

1942—Receives the Spingarn Medal, awarded by the NAACP to African Americans of achievement.

1947—Establishes the League for Nonviolent Civil Disobedience Against Military Segregation.

1948—Protests military segregation at the Democratic National Convention in July; President Harry S. Truman orders integration of the armed forces.

1955—The AFL and CIO unite; Randolph is appointed to the AFL-CIO executive council.

1957—Leads the Prayer Pilgrimage in Washington, D.C., in May.

1958—Leads the Youth March to Integrate Schools on October 25.

1959—A second youth march is held on April 18.

1960—Founds the Negro American Labor Council (NALC) to increase the role of African Americans in organized labor; serves as NALC president through 1966.

1961—The AFL-CIO executive council votes to censure Randolph.

1963—Lucille Randolph dies on April 12; Randolph leads the March on Washington for Jobs and Freedom on August 28.

1964—President Lyndon Johnson presents the Medal of Freedom to Randolph.

1965—With Bayard Rustin, Randolph founds the A. Philip Randolph Institute.

1968—Resigns as president of the Brotherhood of Sleeping Car Porters.

1979—A. Philip Randolph dies on May 16, at age ninety.

CHAPTER NOTES

Chapter 1. One Man's Dream

1. Bayard Rustin, "In Memory of A. Philip Randolph," *American Federationist*, June 1979; reprinted by the A. Philip Randolph Institute.

2. Ibid.

3. "Excerpts from Addresses at Lincoln Memorial During Capital Civil Rights March," *The New York Times*, August 29, 1963, p. C21.

4. Ibid.

5. Ibid.

6. Ibid.

7. Quoted in Phyl Garland, "A. Philip Randolph: Labor's Grand Old Man," *Ebony*, May 1969, p. 34.

8. Ibid.

Chapter 2. Preacher's Son

1. Quoted in Jervis Anderson, *A. Philip Randolph: A Biographical Portrait* (New York: Harcourt Brace Jovanovich, 1973), p. 39.

2. Quoted in Edwin R. Embree, *13 Against the Odds* (New York: Viking Press, 1944), p. 214.

3. Ibid.

4. A. Philip Randolph, "Vita," unpublished manuscript, A. Philip Randolph Collection, Library of Congress, p. 34.

5. Quoted in Michael W. Williams, ed., *The African American Encyclopedia* (New York: Marshall Cavendish, 1993), vol. 6, p. 1589.

6. Randolph, "Vita," p. 4.

7. Quoted in Embree, p. 213.

8. Randolph, "Vita," p. 38.

9. Ibid., p. 12.

10. *Florida Times-Union and Citizen*, May 4, 1901, in Frederick T. Davis, *History of Jacksonville, Florida and Vicinity* (Jacksonville, Fla.: Florida Historical Society, 1925), p. 39.

11. Ibid.

Chapter 3. Coming Into His Own

1. Quoted in John Hope Franklin and Alfred A. Moss, Jr., *From Slavery to Freedom*, 6th ed. (New York: McGraw-Hill, Inc., 1988), p. 246.

2. W. E. B. Du Bois, *The Souls of Black Folk*, in *Writings* (New York: Library of America, 1986), p. 400.

3. W. E. B. Du Bois, "The Talented Tenth: A Memorial Address," in David Levering Lewis, ed., *W. E. B. Du Bois: A Reader* (New York: Henry Holt and Company, 1995), p. 347.

4. Quoted in Jervis Anderson, *A. Philip Randolph: A Biographical Portrait* (New York: Harcourt Brace Jovanovich, 1973), p. 44.

5. A. Philip Randolph, "Vita," unpublished manuscript, A. Philip Randolph Collection, Library of Congress, p. 24.

6. A. Philip Randolph, "If I Were Young Today," *Ebony*, July 1963, p. 82.

7. Ibid.

8. Du Bois, *The Souls of Black Folk*, p. 364.

9. Ibid., p. 391.

10. Quoted in Anderson, p. 52.

11. Ibid., p. 66.

Chapter 4. Socialist

1. Eugene V. Debs, "The Negro Class Struggle," in Jean Y. Tussey, ed., *Eugene V. Debs Speaks* (New York: Pathfinder Press, 1970), p. 93.

2. Ibid., p. 95.

3. Quoted in Jervis Anderson, *A. Philip Randolph: A Biographical Portrait* (New York: Harcourt Brace Jovanovich, 1973), p. 78.

4. *Messenger*, November 1917, p. 21.

5. Ibid.

6. "Negro Mass Movement," *Messenger*, May–June 1919, p. 8.

7. Ibid., p. 9.

8. Ibid.

9. Ibid.

10. A. Philip Randolph, "Lynching: Capitalism Its Cause; Socialism Its Cure," *Messenger*, March 1919, p. 9.

Chapter 5. Dangerous!

1. "The New Patriotism," *Messenger*, November 1917, p. 36.

2. W. E. B. Du Bois, "Close Ranks," in David Levering Lewis, ed., *W. E. B. Du Bois: A Reader* (New York: Henry Holt and Company, 1995), p. 697.

3. "Who Shall Pay for the War," *Messenger*, November 1917, p. 7.

4. "Negro Leaders to Present War Aims to Negroes," *Messenger*, November 1917, p. 8.

5. "New Leadership for the Negro," *Messenger*, May–June 1919, p. 9.

6. Claude McKay, "If We Must Die," *Messenger*, September 1919, p. 4.

7. "The 'New Crowd Negro' Making America Safe for Himself," *Messenger*, September 1919, p. 17.

8. Quoted in Jervis Anderson, *A. Philip Randolph: A Biographical Portrait* (New York: Harcourt Brace Jovanovich, 1973), p. 119.

9. Marcus Garvey, "The Negro's Greatest Enemy," in Cary D. Wintz, ed., *African American Political Thought, 1890–1930* (Armonk, N.Y.: M. E. Sharpe, 1996), p. 171.

10. Ibid.

11. Quoted in Paula F. Pfeffer, *A. Philip Randolph, Pioneer of the Civil Rights Movement* (Baton Rouge, La.: Louisiana State University Press, 1990), p. 16.

12. Quoted in Anderson, p. 143.

13. Ibid., p. 153.

Chapter 6. The Brotherhood Is Born

1. A. Philip Randolph, "Pullman Porters Need Own Union," *Messenger*, August 1925, p. 306.

2. Quoted in Jervis Anderson, *A. Philip Randolph: A Biographical Portrait* (New York: Harcourt Brace Jovanovich, 1973), p. 168.

3. Quoted in John L. Papanek, ed., *African Americans: Voices of Triumph—Leadership* (Alexandria, Va.: Time Life Books, 1994), p. 84.

4. A. Philip Randolph, "To the Brotherhood Men," *Messenger,* March 1926, p. 90.

5. A. Philip Randolph, Letter to Milton P. Webster, September 17, 1926. Records of the Brotherhood of Sleeping Car Porters. Holdings of the Chicago Historical Society and the Newberry Library, Series A, Part 1.

6. A. Philip Randolph, Letter to Milton P. Webster, September 20, 1926. Records of the Brotherhood of Sleeping Car Porters. Holdings of the Chicago Historical Society and the Newberry Library, Series A, Part 1.

7. Ibid.

8. A. Philip Randolph, "Our Next Step," *Messenger*, April 1928, p. 90.

Chapter 7. Victory

1. Quoted in Jervis Anderson, *A. Philip Randolph: A Biographical Portrait* (New York: Harcourt Brace Jovanovich, 1973), p. 203.

2. Quoted in Nell Irvin Painter, "Black Workers from Reconstruction to the Great Depression," in Paul Buhle and Alan Dawley, eds., *Working for Democracy: American Workers from the Revolution to the Present* (Urbana, Ill.: University of Illinois Press, 1985), p. 68.

3. Quoted in Sally Hanley, *A. Philip Randolph: Labor Leader* (New York: Chelsea House Publishers, 1989), p. 71.

4. Quoted in Painter, p. 64.

5. Quoted in Philip S. Foner, *Organized Labor and the Black Worker, 1619–1981* (New York: International Publishers, 1982), p. 188.

6. Quoted in Anderson, p. 214.

7. Quoted in Jack Santino, *Miles of Smiles, Years of Struggle* (Urbana, Ill.: University of Illinois Press, 1989), p. 48.

8. Ibid.

Chapter 8. The Will to Struggle

1. Phyl Garland, "A. Philip Randolph: Labor's Grand Old Man," *Ebony*, May 1969, p. 33.

2. Nell Irvin Painter, "Black Workers from Reconstruction to the Great Depression," in Paul Buhle and Alan Dawley, eds., *Working for Democracy: American Workers from the Revolution to the Present* (Urbana, Ill.: University of Illinois Press, 1985), p. 70.

3. Quoted in Paula F. Pfeffer, *A. Philip Randolph, Pioneer of the Civil Rights Movement* (Baton Rouge, La.: University of Louisiana Press, 1990), p. 35.

4. Quoted in Jervis Anderson, *A. Philip Randolph: A Biographical Portrait* (New York: Harcourt Brace Jovanovich, 1973), p. 296.

5. Quoted in Jacqueline Jones, *American Work: Four Centuries of Black and White Labor* (New York: W. W. Norton and Co., 1998), p. 345.

6. Ibid.

7. Quoted in Edwin R. Embree, *13 Against the Odds* (New York: Viking Press, 1944), p. 227.

8. Quoted in Pfeffer, p. 47.

9. Quoted in Anderson, p. 248.

10. Ibid.

11. Quoted in Pfeffer, p. 47.

12. Quoted in Anderson, p. 251.

13. "A. Philip Randolph's Call for a March," in Albert Fried, ed., *Except to Walk Free: Documents and Notes in the History of American Labor* (Garden City, N.Y.: Anchor Books, 1974), p. 259.

14. Ibid.

15. Ibid.

16. Quoted in Allan Morrison, "A. Philip Randolph: Dean of Negro Leaders," *Ebony*, November 1958, p. 106.

17. Ibid., p. 108.

Chapter 9. Labor's Conscience

1. Quoted in Jervis Anderson, *A. Philip Randolph: A Biographical Portrait* (New York: Harcourt Brace Jovanovich, 1973), p. 275.

2. Ibid., p. 276.

3. Ibid.

4. Ibid.

5. Lucille Randolph, telegram to A. Philip Randolph, April 1, 1948. Brotherhood of Sleeping Car Porters Collection, Library of Congress, Box 105.

6. Anderson, p. 279.

7. Quoted in Charles M. Christian, *Black Saga* (Boston: Houghton Mifflin Co., 1995), p. 378.

8. Ibid.

9. Quoted in Anderson, p. 282.

10. Ibid.

11. Quoted in Joseph C. Goulden, *Meany* (New York: Atheneum, 1972), p. 206.

12. Ibid., p. 309.

13. Ibid., p. 307.

14. Quoted in Murray Kempton, "A. Philip Randolph: *The Choice, Mr. President . . . ,*" *New Republic*, July 6, 1963, p. 16.

15. Quoted in Anderson, p. 304.

16. Quoted in Allan Morrison, "A. Philip Randolph: Dean of Negro Leaders," *Ebony*, November 1958, p. 112.

Chapter 10. Generations

1. Quoted in Jervis Anderson, *A. Philip Randolph: A Biographical Portrait* (New York: Harcourt Brace Jovanovich, 1973), p. 18.

2. Quoted in *A. Philip Randolph: For Jobs and Freedom* (WETA/PBS-TV biography) <http://www.pbs.org/weta/apr> (August 3, 2000).

3. Ibid.

4. Quoted in Paula E. Pfeffer, *A. Philip Randolph, Pioneer of the Civil Rights Movement* (Baton Rouge, La.: Louisiana State University Press, 1990), p. 244.

5. Quoted in Murray Kempton, "A. Philip Randolph: *The Choice, Mr. President . . . ,*" *New Republic*, July 6, 1963, p. 17.

6. Quoted in Anderson, p. 327.

7. Quoted in James Haskins, *The March on Washington* (New York: HarperCollins Publishers, 1993), p. 77.

8. Quoted in *A. Philip Randolph: For Jobs and Freedom*.

9. "Excerpts from Addresses at Lincoln Memorial During Capital Civil Rights March," *The New York Times*, August 29, 1963, p. C21.

10. Quoted in Haskins, pp. 71–73.

11. Quoted in Pfeffer, p. 257.

12. Quoted in Haskins, p. 112.

13. Quoted in Phyl Garland, "A. Philip Randolph: Labor's Grand Old Man," *Ebony*, May 1969, p. 36.

14. Quoted in Kwame Anthony Appiah and Henry Louis Gates, Jr., eds., *Africana* (New York: Basic Civitas Books, 1999), p. 260.

15. Quoted in Charles M. Christian, *Black Saga* (Boston: Houghton Mifflin Co., 1995), p. 429.

16. Quoted in Garland, p. 32.

17. Ibid., p. 31.

18. Quoted in Anderson, p. 349.

19. Ibid., p. 348.

20. A. Philip Randolph, "If I Were Young Today," *Ebony*, July 1963, p. 82.

FURTHER READING

Hanley, Sally. *A. Philip Randolph: Labor Leader.* New York: Chelsea House, 1989.

Harris, William H. *Keeping the Faith: A. Philip Randolph, Milton Webster and the Brotherhood of Sleeping Car Porters.* Urbana, Ill.: University of Illinois Press, 1977, 1991.

Haskins, James. *Bayard Rustin: Behind the Scenes of the Civil Rights Movement.* New York: Hyperion Books for Children, 1997.

———. *The March on Washington.* New York: HarperCollins, 1993.

McKissack, Patricia, and Fredrick McKissack. *A Long Hard Journey: The Story of the Pullman Porter.* New York: Walker and Company, 1989.

Patterson, Lillie. *A. Philip Randolph: Messenger for the Masses.* New York: Facts On File, 1995.

Wright, Sarah. *A. Philip Randolph: Integration in the Workplace.* Englewood Cliffs, N.J.: Silver Burdett Press, 1990.

INTERNET ADDRESSES

A. Philip Randolph: For Jobs and Freedom
<http://www.pbs.org/weta/apr>
Based on a 1998 documentary produced for public television, this site provides information on the life and work of A. Philip Randolph; the essay "In Search of A. Philip Randolph," by Juan Williams; and links to Web sites on African-American history and the labor movement.

A. Philip Randolph/Pullman Porter Museum
<http://www.wimall.com/pullportermu>
Displays photographs from the historical collection of this Chicago museum and offers information on the history of the Pullman porter.

A. Philip Randolph Institute
<http://www.aprihq.org>
Site includes biographical notes on A. Philip Randolph and Bayard Rustin and spells out the goals of the institute.

INDEX

Page numbers for photographs are in **boldface** type.

Randolph, Lucille Campbell
   Green (wife), 39–41, **40**, 42,
   54, 55, 73, 92, 101–102
Reuther, Walter, **8**, 104–105
Rockwell, George Lincoln, 106
Roosevelt, Eleanor, 85
Roosevelt, Franklin Delano, 73,
   81, 83, 85, 103
Rustin, Bayard, 11, 13, 90–92,
   94, 105, 111, **112**, 113

S
segregation, 23–24
Socialist Party; socialism, 36–37,
   42–44, 47, 52
strikes, 37–38, **38**, 70–71
Student Nonviolent
   Coordinating Committee
   (SNCC), 13

T
Thomas, Norman, 52
Totten, Ashley, 55–56, 60, 61, 63
Townsend, Willard, 96

Truman, Harry S., 90, 92, 93
Turner, Henry McNeal, 18–19
Tuskegee Institute, 26

U
Universal Negro Improvement
   Association, 53, 54

V
Voting Rights Act of 1965, 108

W
Walker, Madam C. J., 39
Washington, D.C., 7, 81, 84
Washington, Booker T., 26–27,
   31, 34
Webster, Milton, 63, 66, 69, 71,
   83
White, Walter F., 81
Wilkins, Roy, **8**, 13, **99**
World War I, 45–47
World War II, 80, 86–87

Y
Young, Whitney M., Jr., **8**, 13